FLR

Small Claims
Made Easy

Veronica Newman

Small Claims
by Veronica Newman

Published by
Lawpack Publishing Limited
76–89 Alscot Road
London SE1 3AW

www.lawpack.co.uk

© 2006 Lawpack Publishing

ISBN: 1-904053-75-0
ISBN: 978-1-904053-75-0

Crown copyright material is reproduced with the permission of the Controller of HMSO and the Queen's Printer for Scotland.

Exclusion of Liability and Disclaimer

While every effort has been made to ensure that this Lawpack publication provides accurate and expert guidance, it is impossible to predict all the circumstances in which it may be used. Accordingly, neither the publisher, author, retailer, nor any other suppliers shall be liable to any person or entity with respect to any loss or damage caused or alleged to be caused by the information contained in or omitted from this Lawpack publication.

For convenience (and for no other reason) 'him', 'he' and 'his' have been used throughout and should be read to include 'her', 'she' and 'her'.

Contents

About the author

Veronica Newman was called to the Bar by Gray's Inn in 1984. Following pupillage in London Chambers she practised in Manchester Chambers, covering a broad range of common law claims. After private practice at the Bar she worked for two firms of solicitors, first in Manchester and then for a national law firm at their Cardiff office. Later, she worked as a university lecturer in law. She has now returned to legal practice as a sole practitioner. Veronica lives in Cardiff with her husband, Paul, and their two sons.

Thanks and dedication

Thanks to my editor, who trusted me to write this book. Thanks to my husband, Paul, who proofread the script. Finally to our boys, David and Jonathan, who put up with overcooked dinners and the preoccupation of their mum!

CHAPTER 1

The importance of access to justice

When providers of goods and services appear unwilling to take our complaints seriously, our rights are only as strong as our ability to enforce them. As informed consumers, we know a raft of consumer legislation protects us. However, our ability to rectify the problems that can arise depends upon the willingness of providers of goods and services to acknowledge our rights.

Using a solicitor

If you are planning to enforce your rights, you may think about asking a solicitor to take up your case, but a solicitor's time can be charged out at anything from £90 to £500 an hour. For a small claim under £5,000 it simply does not make economic sense to ask a lawyer to act for us. What matters then is how to gain access to justice, when, for example:

- your builder does not complete the work on your home properly;

- your landlord will not return your deposit;

- the neighbours have built their new garden wall on your land;

- the pre-owned car you purchased has broken down with numerous faults;

- your customer has not paid you for goods or services you delivered to them;

- you injured yourself on some slippery stairs in a pub that were not illuminated properly and you were off work for two weeks with a sprained ankle;

- the dry cleaner ruined your best designer dress.

Naturally, you attempt to settle with your builder or landlord or finance company or customer or insurer amicably. If this fails, you can try to walk away and forget about the matter and put it down to experience, unless you are actually being asked to pay money you do not consider you owe. But if you cannot settle and you cannot walk away, what can you do?

Debt recovery agencies

There are a number of reputable debt recovery agencies that carry out business online which can assist you. Debt recovery agencies understand that most debtors, when faced with a chasing letter and threat of legal action, pay up. Some agencies operate a commission charging system and others charge a flat rate for each stage of the process. Unfortunately, you cannot recover the cost of using a debt recovery agency from the defendant, so the cost will come directly out of your pocket.

If the debtor does not pay and you have to make a claim in the County Court, the debt recovery agency will make the claim on your behalf. Many agencies begin claims at the Bulk Claim Production Centre of the Northampton County Court. It is located on an industrial estate near Northampton and operates a user-friendly service called Money Claim Online (MCOL). **But anyone who has access to a computer can use Money Claim Online.**

If you look at chapter 6, you can read about how the service operates. Whether you instruct a debt recovery agency, or pursue your debtor online or in your local County Court personally, any claim under £5,000 will proceed through the Small Claims Court.

The Small Claims Court

All cases that begin in the County Court are broadly divided into three categories:

- Cases where the claim is under £5,000, i.e. small claims.
- Cases where the claim is over £5,000 but below £15,000.
- Cases where the claim is above £15,000.

All cases that are small claims are put on what is called the 'small claims track'. This means that they will progress along a route to trial designed specifically for low-value cases.

What is the Small Claims Court?

It is not a separate part of the County Court. The Small Claims Court really describes the way in which cases below £5,000 are processed. The idea behind it is that claims under £5,000 should be heard in a way that allows the public to make claims without a lawyer.

All County Court claims are processed in accordance with a set of rules called the Civil Procedure Rules 1998. The rules that apply to small claims state that even those who win their cases will not be allowed to recover the full cost of taking legal action from the other side. This is because the Small Claims Court is designed to discourage people from using lawyers at the hearings, as it is more for the layperson.

The place of the hearing is not a court of the type you may have seen on television. It is not like the local Magistrates' Court either. It is more like an office and everyone in it will sit down to speak to the District Judge. They will not stand up and make speeches. This does not mean that lawyers cannot represent anyone in the Small Claims Court. However, as the cost of a solicitor or a barrister cannot be awarded to the winner at the trial, they are far less likely to make an appearance in the Small Claims Court.

How this book can help

This book is designed to help you access the Small Claims Court and to lead you through the process step by step. If the book refers to any legal terms, the meaning is explained. There is a Glossary at the end of the book to help. The steps are illustrated with examples based on real cases, although the names and personalities of the characters are fictitious.

The book will show you how to fill in the forms, to get your claim started, and how your case will progress. The contents listing is intended to guide you to the section most relevant to what you are doing. Obviously, if you have already obtained a judgment but you now need to get your money out of a reluctant debtor, you can go straight to chapter 8. You can explore other ways to avoid going to court in chapter 2.

Note: This book covers many aspects of civil claims but the following are outside the scope of this book.

- Fast track cases
- 'Multi-track' cases
- Employment law
- Criminal matters
- Land law claims
- Wills and probate

Who the book can help

This book will assist anyone who needs to recover money from a person or organisation that has not delivered goods or services that should have been delivered or who has suffered loss as a result of another person's or organisation's conduct.

You may be an individual or a sole trader or a very small limited company. You may be a club or voluntary organisation. You may have suffered a minor accident at work. Your customer may not have paid you for the building work you carried out at his home, the repairs to his motor car, the

4Walls invoice

Date: 2 February 2006

Brian and Carol Clarke
Sheiling Lawn Cottage
Bays Lane
Oxon OX9 3PP

4Walls Maintenance Company Ltd
2 Tracey Drive
Horn Lane
Oxon OX5 7AP
Email: 4walls@homenet.co.uk
Tel: 01632 235 978
Fax: 01632 235 979

Item	Item Description	Unit Price	Total Price
1	Removing and rebedding two leaking roof panels and applying 'mastic' sealant		£90.00
2	Applying 'mastic' window sealant to the exterior of the windows		£50.00
3	Removing and resiting hinges on double door and rehanging doors		£250.00
4	Hacking off and reapplying 2.5m of plaster under windows		£380.00
5	Removing defective handle on fanlight window and replacing all windows and doors with new matching fittings (old handles no longer available)		£245.00
Net price			£1,015.00
VAT			£177.63
Total			**£1,192.63**

new crown you fitted to his tooth, the repair you carried out on the kitchen appliances. This book can help all kinds of claimants.

You may also be a householder dissatisfied with minor building works, repairs or alterations, like Brian and Carol below:

Brian is a Junior Manager with a high-street clothing store. He earns regular reasonable money and his prospects are good, but he cannot afford to waste money either.

Carol, his wife, is a qualified nursery nurse and she works part time to fit in with the school hours and holidays of their two children, aged five and three years old.

In October 2005 they engaged a builder to install and erect a conservatory at the rear of their house. They needed the extra space so that the children's toys could be moved out of the living room as they felt that they needed one adult uncluttered space. There was no written contract, but the builder prepared an estimate dated 11 October 2005.

After it was built, Brian and Carol found out that the conservatory had two leaks in the roof panels, a leaky double door letting in rain from the garden, plaster under a window was cracking and 'blown' from water seeping in from the outside, and the handle on the fanlight window would not lock.

When Brian spoke to the builder, George Biddulph, about it, he was sympathetic at first and said he would take a look at it, but he never showed up. Eventually, Brian and Carol got another builder to put right all the defects. They sent George Biddulph a copy of the bill and asked him to pay it. A copy of the bill from 4Walls Maintenance Company Ltd is shown on the previous page.

On receipt of the bill, George Biddulph spoke to Brian and said that there was nothing wrong with his work and he would not pay the cost of the repair.

What did Brian and Carol do next? They went to see a local solicitor who wrote them the letter on the following page.

We will come back to Brian and Carol later, but the letter they received from their solicitor illustrates the problem of trying to get **a lawyer to**

Example solicitor's letter

Dawson Jacobs & Co, Swindon
Tel: 01632 326 971

21 February 2006

Mr Brian Clarke
Sheiling Lawn Cottage
Bays Lane
Oxon OX9 3PP

Dear Mr and Mrs Clarke,

Our Ref: 04/236784

We refer to our recent meeting at our offices.

- We regret that we are unable to act for you in your claim for the cost of putting right the defects to your conservatory. Your claim for £1,192.63 amounts to a small claim, i.e. less than £5,000. If we were successful in recovering your money, we would only be able to claim the cost of issuing the court document, called the Claim Form, and a maximum of £50 for your witness, the trader who carried out your repairs.

- Your claim is for just under £1,200, but we anticipate we would have to charge approximately £1,800 to represent you since we charge our junior fee earners out at £85 per hour. Under the court rules, you are not entitled to recover that sum from George Biddulph, if you win the case.

- We suggest that you try to talk to Mr Biddulph yourself and come to some kind of compromise. If this is not possible, you can represent yourself at the Small Claims Court of your local County Court. The court has a booklet designed to help you get started, although the court staff cannot give you legal advice. Your local County Court is the Swindon County Court.

- Alternatively, you could try checking your household insurance to see if you have legal expenses cover that would entitle you to legal representation.

Naturally, we wish you every success.

Yours sincerely,

Andrew Jacobs

deal with a small claim. Unfortunately, their household insurance only covered them for defending a claim by the builder and not for making a claim against the builder.

What claims can you take to the Small Claims Court?

Claim	Example
Any claim where the financial value is £5,000 or less.	Ellen made a pair of curtains for her customer, Mrs Fenchurch. Ellen relied on Mrs Fenchurch's measurements for the windows. Mrs Fenchurch has cancelled the cheque for £2,500 that she gave to Ellen to pay for them, because she claims that they are too short.
Any claim for personal injuries where the claim for the physical or mental injury to a person is less than £1,000.	Beverly tripped up over a pile of files that had been left on the floor and not filed. Beverly landed awkwardly and twisted her ankle. The pain was so bad that she went to the casualty unit of the local hospital where she was told that her ankle was sprained and she should rest at home for a week. Beverly was prescribed anti-inflammatory drugs to settle the swelling and Paracetamol for the pain.
Any claim for personal injuries where the claim for the damages that are non-personal, i.e. loss of earnings, is less than £5,000.	Beverly had to travel to hospital for two outpatient appointments with the physiotherapist. During the fall her spectacles fell off and her bifocal lenses broke. Her

	estimate of her losses is £100 for the lenses and £30 taxi fares to the hospital. Beverly, who is employed as a clerical assistant in an office, lost £200 in wages.
Any claim by a tenant of residential premises against his landlord to carry out repairs or other work to the premises, where the estimated cost of the repairs is less than £1,000.	Wayne and his girlfriend rent a flat for 12 months. For the past three months their landlord has failed to repair a leak through the bathroom ceiling caused by a leaky pipe in the roof space above. The ceiling is sagging. Wayne brought in a builder who told him it would cost £600 to repair the leak, take down the old plaster and lath ceiling, replace it with plaster board and then apply Artex and repaint the new ceiling.
Any other claim by a tenant against the landlord of residential premises where the financial value is less than £1,000.	Wayne and his girlfriend want money compensation for the inconvenience and vexation they have suffered.

Who can present a case to the Small Claims Court?

- A person who makes a claim and a person who defends a claim can represent themselves.

- A lawyer can represent a person who is making or defending a claim.

- An employee of a limited company can represent his employer.

- A layperson can represent another person who is making or defending a claim, but only as long as the claimant gives evidence to the District Judge.

Let us see how this last rule works out in practice by looking at Ray's problem.

'I'm Ray, a time-served master upholsterer. I've got lots of good customers and I run a workshop with three qualified upholsterers. I've been successful, mainly because I don't get involved in anything that keeps me away from actually doing my job.

My wife writes the letters on the computer and makes my appointments with the customers. She also deals with telephone queries. We also have a book-keeper called Brenda, a friend of my wife, who sends out the invoices and does the debt chasing.

Upholstering one three-piece suite of furniture can cost our customer £3,000, but a large part of the cost is the fabric to cover the suite. So, having purchased the fabric at upwards of £20 per metre, we cannot afford to wait long for payment. Mostly we have good customers, all round the South East, but we do get the odd one that we have to sue.

We do not employ Brenda. We buy in her services and she has other customers like us, but she knows our business through and through. You see, it is Brenda who really deals with the debt chasing. There is nothing I can tell the court about it and I can't afford to be spending time in court.

When we have to take a non-payer to court can Brenda represent us?'

The answer is 'yes'. Brenda can represent Ray, but he would still have to attend court to tell the judge about the case. This is because only Ray has the right to ask the court to give him a judgment against a customer if he can prove that:

- he made a contract with his customer on agreed terms;
- he did the work;
- the customer did not pay him;
- he has suffered a loss as a result of the customer not paying him.

Only Ray can give evidence about the agreement he made with the customer since it is he who contracted with the customer. Only Ray can tell the court that the furniture was upholstered in the fashion agreed since it is he who has overall control of the fabrication process involved. Only Brenda can tell the court about any efforts she made to chase up the debt and what response she has got from the customer. This is because it was Brenda who chased up the debt. Anything Ray knows about Brenda's efforts to chase up the debts is not his direct knowledge, but what Brenda has told Ray or Ray's wife. Although Brenda can present Ray's case to the court, Ray would still have to attend. He can avoid going to court to give evidence if the debtor confirms that he agrees with Ray's evidence and confirms to Brenda and the court that he does not wish to question Ray.

Who hears a small claim?

The District Judge hears the case. He is usually a solicitor or a barrister who has been specially trained to hear low-value, but important, cases. 'Low-value' generally means less than £5,000. The District Judge does not wear robes or a wig. He wears ordinary professional clothes. The District Judge speaks in plain language so that everyone can understand what is happening. The District Judge does not expect either party to argue about the law because neither of the people in his court room are lawyers. He will decide what law is relevant to the case based on the facts that each side brings to his attention. Then he will apply the law to the facts of each case and reach a decision.

Things you need to consider before you get started

Will the debtor pay you?

If you are successful in obtaining a judgment, will you be paid? Most debtors will pay a judgment debt rather than endure appearing on a bad debtor's list or the Register of Judgments, Orders and Fines. This is because the ability to obtain credit is affected by being on these lists. Not all debtors worry about it, though. Before you embark on a claim you need to be clear about the likelihood of being paid in the end. This is because you will have to pay court fees before the court office will issue the Claim Form. You will pay another fee before the court office will give you a trial date. You will have to take time off work to attend court to present your case to the District Judge during your precious working hours. Then there is the anxiety that making or defending a claim can cause. You can waste money unless your debtor pays up, so claims should not be undertaken lightly.

Why debtors do not pay debts or judgments

- They simply cannot pay.
- They are owed money by their customers and are awaiting payment themselves.
- The debtor **feels** that there is a genuine partial or total defence.

Checking out an individual

If you suspect that your debtor cannot pay because he is in financial difficulty, you must try to find out whether your debtor is likely to go bust before you can enforce any judgment of the court. You can check the Register of Judgments, Orders and Fines by visiting www.registry-trust.org.uk. Alternatively, you can write to the registry at Registry Trust Limited, 173–175 Cleveland Street, London W1T 6QR or you can telephone them on 020 7380 0133.

If your debtor has unpaid County Court judgments, then you will need to consider whether you are any more likely to be paid than the other creditors.

If your debtor has ceased trading, you can find out if he is already personally insolvent (bankrupt) by visiting www.insolvency.gov.uk where you can carry out a search online to check if the debtor is already bankrupt or facing bankruptcy proceedings.

Doing a company search

If your debtor is a company, you can do a company search to see if the company has assets out of which it can pay your judgment debt. You can find this out by writing to Companies House, Crown Way, Cardiff CF14 3UZ. Alternatively, visit its website at www.companies-house.gov.uk.

If you suspect that your debtor may have a genuine reason for not paying up, then look at chapter 2, which focuses on how to avoid court.

What it costs to claim against a debtor

The court charges for its services in administering the claim. This is because the court occupies buildings maintained by the taxpayer and employs staff to carry out the administration of civil justice. The cost currently depends upon how much money you are claiming. The more money you are claiming the higher the fees the court charges. Here is a table of the fees charged as of April 2006 to begin a claim in the Small Claims Court.

Size of claim	Court fee
Under £300	£30
Between £300 and £500	£50
Between £500 and £1,000	£80
Between £1,000 and £5,000	£120

Whether you are entitled to an exemption from payment of court fees

The whole point of the Small Claims Court is to ensure that those with small claims are able to get access to civil justice. Consequently, the court rules permit claimants or defendants who have to pay a court fee to apply for an exemption or reduction of the fees. To find out if you qualify for an exemption or remission of court fees, you can pick up leaflet EX160A from any County Court office or online at www.hmcourts-service.gov.uk.

The court can also reduce or remit the fees for small claims proceedings if payment would cause undue financial hardship. Applicants for exemption from or remission of the court fees must complete Form EX160A, available from any County Court office or online at www.hmcourts-service.gov.uk/infoabout/fees. The form requires information about the applicant's personal details, income and expenses and you must be able to produce documents to verify what you say on the form. No application will be considered until those documents are produced.

Those court users who have already paid a court fee but who are exempt can apply for a refund by completing Form EX160. Applications for a refund must be made within six months of paying the fee.

Once the completed application form and verifying documents are returned to the court office the court can decide whether:

- you should not pay a fee; or
- you should pay a smaller fee; or
- you must pay the whole fee.

Should you be unhappy with the decision you can appeal against it, but you must do so within 14 days of receiving the court's letter notifying you of the decision.

Other costs

Apart from the issue fee there are other costs to consider. If you need witnesses to give evidence, they will have expenses to attend court and perhaps loss of earnings. If you are successful and win your case, the court can order the other side to pay the following:

- Your witness expenses. These would include the cost of travelling to the court and/or staying overnight away from home and loss of earnings. The sum is limited to £50 per day per person. There is little incentive for someone who earns more than £50 per day to come voluntarily to court and it may be necessary to issue a witness summons to ensure that the witness attends court to give evidence. There is a witness summons fee of £35 as of 6 April 2006, but you need to check with the court how much it is as the fees are revised from time to time. The Court Service website also gives information on what the fees are.

- Your own expenses in travelling to court, including overnight expenses and loss of earnings.

- Expert witness expenses of up to £200.

The costs if you lose

If you lose, the other side will be entitled to claim their loss of earnings, travel expenses, witnesses travel and loss of earnings and expert witness costs, if any.

If you have legal expenses insurance

Some household insurance policies provide legal expenses cover and some professional or trade association memberships carry benefits, such as legal expenses insurance. It is always worth checking these to see if the insurer can meet the costs of using a solicitor.

Starting a claim in any court should not be done lightly, so in the next chapter the alternatives are explored.

CHAPTER 2

Avoiding court

The most sensible thing anyone with a claim against someone can do is to try to settle it before the dispute becomes 'septic'. Most people understand this, but sometimes it is difficult to know how to complain in a way that will make people take it seriously. So if it cannot be resolved by informal means, you need to make it formal. Formality is often what will get a claim taken seriously because there is a record of it.

Make your claim formal

There are several ways of making claims: by letter, meetings, telephone calls or email. Whatever method you use, you must:

1. state your name and address;

2. know or find out to whom to address your claim;

3. state the facts leading to the claim – who, what, why, where, when and how;

4. state the facts of the claim, what happened and how it was dealt with at the time;

5. state the action required to resolve the claim and how long you expect it to take.

Telephone calls

These are very hard to ignore. If you get through to the person you wish to speak to, it is your opportunity to get the other side to deal sympathetically with your complaint. There are no visual impressions to distract the listener from what you actually say. It can be an immediate way of bringing the matter to the attention of the correct person and you do not have to travel anywhere, saving precious time.

As with any other formal meeting you need to prepare by ensuring that you have all the documents and facts to hand before you pick up the receiver. You also need to begin with your name, your position and what you are calling about. Get the other person to confirm that he is able to deal with your call and then relate the facts and ask for what you want clearly and firmly. Sometimes just asking for what you want may be all that is needed to resolve your complaint.

Try to approach telephone calls in the manner of someone genuinely trying to resolve issues. Your debtor may have a genuine good reason for failing to pay and a telephone conversation may lead to a resolution of the problem. However, if your debtor is simply trying to avoid payment with promises of 'a cheque in the post', you need to tie him down to a firm commitment to make a payment by a fixed date. If your debtor is not listening, then you must politely but firmly inform him of his obligations, say how he can meet those obligations, by what time and date and what you will do if they are not met.

If you use the telephone, you should follow up with something in writing setting out a summary of what was said and what was agreed, if anything. This could be a letter or email to your debtor confirming the conversation. Alternatively, you could keep a record known as an attendance note. This is a record used by solicitors, but it can be used by anybody. An example can be found on the following page.

Remember to time your telephone calls carefully. If you telephone someone at 12.55, the operative is mentally already on his lunch break and he may deal with you quicker so he can get away to lunch. Similarly, if a person dealing with your complaint goes into work knowing you will be on the telephone the minute he gets to his desk at 08.30, he is more likely to get on and deal with it. It is simply human nature to want to get a complaining customer 'off your back'.

Example attendance note

Date: 16 November 2006

Time: 1445

Who: ABC Bank Limited

Subject: Charges on current account

Spoke with Mrs Merkin of ABC, who apologised for not getting back to me sooner, but she had had to look into the facts set out in my letter of 2 November. She said that the charges made against our account should not have been made and that the bank would be crediting the charges to our account.

I asked how soon it would happen and she confirmed that the transfer would take place tomorrow. I said that I would be checking my account balance tomorrow to make sure that the credit arrived and would be back on the phone to her if it did not.

Remember to record the contents of any telephone discussion and any agreement made in a note. Alternatively, make an attendance note like the one above. Good record keeping is essential for making sure you are certain about your facts. If it is necessary to go to court, you then have useful evidence that you tried to effect a settlement of your claim.

Meetings

Physically meeting someone can be a good way of resolving a claim. However, the same rules apply. You must give your name, say why you are at the meeting and what you want. Let us look at the following example:

Tim bought a bottle of expensive wine from his local supermarket. Tim's dinner guests decided it 'tasted like cough medicine' and did not drink it. Tim took the bottle back to the store. The wine department manager asked if the wine was 'corked'. Tim said it was not but just 'tasted awful'. The supermarket agreed that in the matter of the taste of wine the customer was always right. The supermarket offered him the opportunity of a refund or to select an alternative bottle at the same price as the original.

You need to ensure that you are speaking to a person with the power to resolve your claim. If you find that you are not, then insist on arranging a further meeting shortly with the correct person. You can complain that you are being 'given the run around', which many organisations find a hard criticism to take. However, sometimes a delay can be turned to your advantage:

Edmund and Karen bought a pushchair from a store. After only six months the wheels cracked and fell off. They went to the store carrying their 11-month-old baby and the original box for the pushchair. It was a busy Saturday afternoon. They explained why they had come and asked to see someone who could help. The Deputy Manager arrived and said that the pushchair was one of a batch that had all been failing and they would receive a refund. Edmund and Karen said that they would like another pushchair and were shown what was in the store. They selected another pushchair but were told it was £10 more than the one they had originally purchased and that they would have to pay the difference.

Edmund and Karen politely, but firmly, said that they wanted to be compensated and that they were not being compensated because they had lost the benefit of a working pushchair at a lower price. If there were no pushchairs at the lower price in the store, they should receive the next best alternative, even if it was more expensive for the store. They added that they had made a special trip in order to return the pushchair. The Deputy Manager said that she had no authority to give them a more expensive pushchair and that the Manager was not at work and could not be contacted.

Edmund and Karen agreed to come back the following week to see the Manager, provided that the store lent them another pushchair, since they did not have one that could be used now. The Deputy Manager reluctantly agreed and gave them the 'loan pushchair', which was actually a brand new one. The following week Edmund and Karen received a new pushchair at the higher price without having to pay more money to the store.

Sometimes a personal visit is required to get a debt paid. Look at the following example:

> Kevin is a hard-working dentist in a country practice with two other dentists. He has a good client of many years, Stuart. Stuart is never swift to pay his bills, but when Kevin saw from his aged debt list that Stuart had not paid him for three months, he went to see him at his house. Stuart was surprised to see his dentist but faced with seeing him on the doorstep, and anxious to end the visit quickly, produced the necessary cheque in three minutes!

As with telephone calls, follow up any meeting by making a record of what was agreed in either a letter, email or attendance note.

Letters and email

Letters and email are an excellent way of resolving disputes without going to court. Letters give you an opportunity to set out your case without interruption. They have to be read and therefore they absorb the attention of the reader. The reader cannot see or hear you and no aspect of your appearance or manner can distract the reader from what you have to say. Letters are dated and are evidence if going to court cannot be avoided. Sometimes a letter is all that is needed to settle a claim; a letter can also result in your receiving a telephone call that will resolve your claim.

It is easy to write a good letter because good letters all have the same qualities. A claim letter should:

1. show the address of the person writing it;

2. show the address of the person you are writing to;

3. show the date;

4. show any reference number that helps to identify the claim, for example an invoice number;

5. display paragraphs written in plain English that set out:

    - the reason for your letter;

    - the facts of your claim;

Example claim letter 1

**Mr G Simmons, 16 Grange Gardens,
Derwent Drive, Bedford**

Tidy Preowns
Lightheart Industrial Estate
Bedford

10 March 2006

Dear Sir,

Re: Pre-owned Car, Wow J90, Reg No CE51 2XW

1.　　We purchased a pre-owned car from your forecourt on 4 February. Your salesman, John Granger, assured us that the vehicle was free from any serious defect, being only three years old, with one previous owner, and a full service history.

2.　　Regrettably, this is far from the case. Here is a list of what has happened since we purchased it:

- On 11 February, the car went dead when my wife was ferrying our two children to school, only a week after we purchased the car. I was forced to leave work to pick her and our children up and take them onto school. Then I had to arrange for the car to be returned to you. You arranged for a new clutch to be installed because the clutch cable had broken, but the repair took two weeks to effect.

- The vehicle was returned to us, but, once we were home, my wife discovered that there was a huge amount of water which had collected in the floor pan of both rear passenger seats.

- A week after that my wife noticed the exhaust pipe was hanging down from the body of the car. When she returned to your garage, Mr Granger informed her that she would have to pay for a new exhaust to be fitted since the old one had a pinhole in it and the brackets that clamp the exhaust to the floor of the car had corroded. My wife asked about the water in the floor pan. Mr Granger informed her that it was the kind of thing that happened to a car of this age!

- The same day, the DVD player packed up. Mr Granger said that it was not covered by any warranty since we had not purchased an extended warranty from you.

- On 5 March the battery became flat and when recharged failed to retain that charge. We were forced to buy a new battery at a cost of £120.

- On 8 March my wife noticed that there was a rattling noise whenever she started the engine. We took the car to our own garage, which has confirmed that the gearbox is failing and will need to be replaced very soon at a cost of £600.

3. We consider that this number of defects should not have occurred so soon after we purchased a three-year-old vehicle, and that this vehicle was in no fit condition to be sold. We have an engineer's report to confirm what we say.

4. Unless within seven days of the date of this letter you confirm that you will accept the return of the vehicle, and return what we paid you, we will make a claim via Money Claim Online. Naturally, we hope that court can be avoided since we will be seeking our engineer's costs and any other compensation and costs to which we are entitled.

Yours faithfully,

G. Simmons

- the action you require;
- the date by which the action is to be taken;

6. include copies of any documents enclosed in your letter;

7. conclude with the hope that the dispute can be resolved shortly; and

8. say what will happen if you do not get what you are asking for.

Debt recovery agencies have a good strike rate because they know how to write threatening letters that debtors take seriously. But you too can write letters that debtors will take seriously using the example claim letter on pages 22–3.

Be prepared to keep going

Do not give up when the first letter is ignored or the telephone line goes dead before you are connected to the person you need to speak to. Some organisations instruct their staff to ignore initial letters of complaint just to see how seriously the customer takes it! Other organisations are naturally good at losing correspondence! Set short time limits for responses and in your next letter or email refer to their failure to acknowledge your letter/email or telephone call and then repeat your claim. To save the time involved in repeating yourself, put copies of previous letters with the next one. Most people hate having to read more than one side of A4 paper!

Know when to back down

Sometimes you will find that there is a genuine defence to a claim you have made. Be prepared to back down when it is necessary. Look at the example below:

Ian, Aled, Duncan and Harry were students and shared a house together in the town centre, near the university they attended. They had a tenancy agreement with the landlord for six months under the Housing Act 1988. They paid a deposit of £880, which, in accordance with the Housing Act 2004, was placed with an independent bondholder.

Example claim letter 2

15 Esslemont Road, Southsea

Tidy Lets
14 Gardinia Close
Portsmouth PO4 1AD

7 July 2006

Dear Sirs,

I am writing on behalf of myself, Aled, Ian and Harry. We were tenants of your property between 6 January and 5 July 2006, although we actually vacated the property at the end of June in order to return home.

When we went to your office at the end of the tenancy we were surprised and dismayed to learn that you would be opposing the return of the full bond by the bondholder. Ms Ratton stated that the house had been left in a very dirty condition and professional cleaners had been sent to put it in order.

We disagree with what she has said since we all vacuumed our own rooms before we left the house. We assume that there may have been a bit of dust settling between the time we vacated and the end of the tenancy.

If, within seven days of the date of this letter, you have not agreed to the return of the full bond with the bondholder, we shall be forced to take legal proceedings against you.

Yours faithfully,

Duncan

Example response to claim letter 2

**Tidy Lets, 14 Gardinia Close,
Portsmouth PO4 1AD**

Tenant
15 Esslemont Road
Southsea

8 July 2006

Dear Tenant,

Re: Tenancy – 6 January–5 July 2006 – 5 Nelson Road, Southsea

1. Further to your letter of 7 July, we attach a schedule of deductions from the bond which we shall be seeking from the 'bondholder'.

2. When our agent called at the property on 5 July, all the occupants had already vacated and so it was not possible for our agent to take you through the deductions we shall be seeking from the bondholder. We understand, however, that a schedule of 'pre-vacation tenant checks', which is given to all our tenants a week prior to departure, was left at the property in accordance with our standard procedures. Therefore, there should have been no confusion as to what had to be done to leave the property in the state it was in at the start of the tenancy.

3. We attach:

    - the schedule of proposed deductions from the bond;

    - a bill from our caretaker for minor repairs;

    - a bill from professional cleaners together with three quotations for the same work.

4. Provided the threat of court proceedings is dropped, we propose the bondholder sends each of the co-sharers a cheque for the sum

of £112.42, as soon as evidence is provided to show that the utility bills on the property have been paid in accordance with the tenancy agreement. Please confirm by return that you are willing to agree. Please confirm with the bondholder that you agree to this proposal. We have digital video footage of the condition of the property when it was let to you and on the expiry of the tenancy. You are welcome to view this at our offices.

Yours faithfully,

Landlord

Enc.

Example inspection schedule

Inspection schedule of 5 Nelson Road, Southsea, Hants, carried out on 6 July 2006

Item 1: **Sitting room:**
Main light bulb and two candle bulbs not replaced.

One box for cable telephone left behind.

Cobwebs on the coving.

Sofa cushions and armchairs full of crumbs, food debris, coins and popcorn.

New three-piece suite grubby and in need of a professional clean.

Arms of sofa and chairs covered in grime.

All surfaces of window, skirting boards and floor covered in grime and dust.

Charge: Professional clean.

Item 2: **Middle room:**
One pane of glass in left-hand window next to door recently and badly repaired, not by us.

Puttying in pane of glass will have to be done again.

100-watt light bulb replaced with a 60-watt light bulb and will have to be replaced.

The following rubbish was left behind: various catalogues, chimes and pens.

Charge: Professional clean.

Item 3: **Hallway:**
Dining room cabinet put in hall and not returned to the dining room.

Inside there was rubbish: one pen, one string of Christmas tree lights, one old perfume bottle and one flower pot.

Cupboard not polished or dusted.

No light bulb in the hallway.

Window and front door not dusted and dirty.

Example inspection schedule (continued)

Skirting boards and all other surfaces covered in grime and scuffed.

Wallpaper in hallway scratched and torn by the storage of a bicycle.

Charge: Repairs to wallpaper and repainting.

Professional clean.

Amount: £45.00

Item 4: **Dining room:**

Skirting boards dusty, scuffed and not cleaned.

Light bulb missing from the fitting.

Charge: Fitting light bulb.

Professional clean.

Amount: £0.67

Item 5: **Kitchen:**

Front of washing machine not cleaned.

Left side of fridge/freezer covered in grease but not cleaned inside or out.

Freezer not defrosted completely and not cleaned, and there was a huge puddle of water on the floor.

The kitchen bin was dirty.

The fronts of the cupboards were dirty.

Bag of plain flour in the last cupboard and pink plastic box not removed.

Old ice cube tray left behind.

Sink unit dirty.

Dustpan and hand broom filthy.

Sweet wrapper and dead leaf in the plug hole.

Drainer and washing-up bowl filthy.

All surfaces unwashed and in need of top to bottom clean with degreasers.

Oven filled with cooking debris, carbon deposits and grease.

Example inspection schedule (continued)

Charge: Professional clean.

Item 6: **Garden:**

Dustbin in the garden filled with stinking black bin liner full of accumulated water. On pulling the bin bag out of the dustbin the bag split open and putrid contents spilled onto the concrete outside the kitchen door. We cleaned the concrete with proprietary cleaner, a deck brush and hosepipe in order to remove the stench.

Cleaned obstructed drain.

Charge: 2 hours at £4.00 per hour.

Amount: £8.00

Item 7: **Small front bedroom:**

Light bulb missing.

All surfaces dusty.

Charge: Time spent fitting light bulb.

Professional clean.

Amount: £0.67

Item 8: **Large front bedroom:**

Curtain pole removed but old curtain track not put back.

Spots of paint on the carpet.

All surfaces dusty and windows unwashed.

Charge: Time spent retrieving and fixing old curtain pole and putting up curtains: 30 minutes @ £4.00 per hour.

Professional clean.

Amount: £2.00

Item 9: **Large middle bedroom:**

Curtain pole removed and crude attempt to replace curtain track with a plastic one which was originally in the back

Example inspection schedule (continued)

bedroom and therefore does not fit the larger window of the middle room. Plastic track is, in any event, not fixed adequately to support curtains.

Charge: Time spent finding and retrieving old curtain pole from loft and fixing and replacing curtain: 30 minutes @ £4.00 per hour.
Professional clean.

Amount: £2.00

Item 10:   **Back bedroom:**
Light bulb missing.
Curtain track not replaced at all and therefore needs fixing.

Charge: Time spent fixing curtain pole: 30 minutes @ £4.00 per hour.
Professional clean.

Amount: £2.00

Cost of replacement 100-watt light bulbs:	£2.00
Cost of replacement candle 40-watt light bulbs:	£2.50
Cost of cleaning fluid for yard:	£5.50
Total cost of labour @ £4.00 per hour:	£70.34
Cost of professional cleaners for house and carpets and soft furnishings:	£350.00
Total cost of clean and repair:	£430.34
Bond held by landlords:	£880.00
Less deductions:	£430.34
Total:	**£449.66**

At the end of the tenancy they decided to split up because two of them were moving to permanent jobs elsewhere and Aled was moving in with his girlfriend. When they asked for the deposit to be returned, the bondholder informed them that the landlord was opposing the return of the full bond because the property had been left dirty and there were clean-up and other costs to be deducted from the deposit. When the boys spoke to each other by telephone they concluded that they had cleaned up adequately for the type of house it was. Aled's girlfriend said that they should sue the landlord. However, Duncan suggested that they should write to their landlord first.

On the face of it the landlord appears to have acted unfairly. The letter that Duncan sent to their landlord and the landlord's response can be found on page 25 and the landlord's reply can be found on pages 26–7, along with an inspection schedule of the property (pages 28–31).

After reading the landlord's letter the boys decided it was better to accept the deductions and move on. They sent the landlord proof of payment of utility bills and informed the bondholder that they agreed to the return of the balance of the deposit, which was duly paid.

Offering to settle claims

Another way of avoiding going to court is to offer to settle your claim, i.e. to make an agreement with the other side. Look at the example below:

Katherine is a deaf and dumb interpreter who was not paid £200 by the solicitor who used her for his work. The solicitor's firm was a regular client. She found out that going to court would cost her an issue fee of £30. So she then wrote a very strong letter.

The solicitor telephoned Katherine. He explained that his assistant, contrary to office policy, agreed more than the rate he usually paid. Katherine therefore proposed a reduction of her bill of £25 provided that the solicitor paid her within two days. The solicitor agreed and Katherine confirmed their agreement in writing. Her letter can be found on the following page.

Katherine was paid as agreed and she was relieved because she received her money without having to resort to the Small Claims

Example claim letter 3

**Katherine Hardy, 12 Dove Lane,
Dewsbury, Yorkshire**

Mr Blades
Dewsbury Solicitors
Law Road
Dewsbury

7 July 2006

Dear Mr Blades,

Further to my recent letter to you, and our telephone conversation yesterday evening, I confirm as follows:

- I will resubmit my fee note to you and reduce my fee to £175. Please note the attached reduced fee note as agreed.

- You will pay me that sum within two days of today's date, failing which I shall be entitled to judgment in the Small Claims Court for the full amount.

I look forward to receiving payment.

Yours sincerely,

Katherine Hardy

Enc.

Court. The solicitor felt that he had been listened to because he received the reduction he sought. More importantly, he decided that he would continue to use Katherine's services.

Other alternatives to proceeding in the courts

A number of trade organisations have well-established complaints procedures aimed at resolving disputes between service providers and their customers. You can find a list of organisations that offer complaints handling in the Appendix. Since many enterprises rely on repeat business with their customers, they see sense in resolving complaints at an early stage. Many enterprises regard a proper complaints procedure as the 'Kitemark' of a confident, accessible, customer-focused business. Many businesses see complaints as inevitable and an opportunity to iron out 'glitches' in service delivery.

The Dental Complaints Panel

At a time when NHS dentists are becoming harder to find and patients bow to the inevitable and seek private treatment, the British Dental Council has responded to the service delivery issues, introducing its own complaints handling process. The Dental Complaints Service was launched on 24 May 2006 to encourage dispute resolution between patient and dental health practitioner. The focus is on settling complaints in a non-adversarial way in order to restore the relationship between the parties.

How the scheme works

Patient and dental care practitioner are invited to attend a Complaints Panel, near to where the patient lives. The meetings are arranged in hotel rooms. The panels are composed of three people. One person is a dentist from outside the area in which the patient's dental care practitioner practises. The other two people are ordinary (lay) members of the panel trained to hear complaints fairly. One of the laypeople acts as the Chairman of the Panel and he conducts the meeting. The panel can:

- decide that no further action should be taken because the complaint is not justified;

- make recommendations to the dental care practitioner as to future practice;

- recommend that the dental care professional apologise to the patient and/or offer compensation in the form of a refund and/or a contribution towards remedial treatment;

- make other recommendations.

However, the aim of the panel is to get the dental care practitioner and the patient to arrive at a common understanding of the issues and then to forge their own solution to it. The process is informal and everyone sits around the same table. Both patient and dental care practitioner have an opportunity to tell the panel their version of events. In the event of a settlement of the dispute, the panel draws up a memorandum of agreement. The panel can only make recommendations but if the dental care practitioner fails to follow the recommendations, then the patient may raise the matter with the Dental Complaints Service (DCS). The DCS may then refer the matter to the British Dental Council for disciplinary action. Full details of the scheme can be accessed at www.dentalcomplaints.org.uk.

The Association of Master Upholsterers and Soft Furnishers Arbitration Scheme

The Association of Master Upholsterers and Soft Furnishers (AMUSF) runs both a mediation and an arbitration scheme designed to help its members to resolve disputes with customers. The scheme is free to the consumer. The member pays the association's charges for providing the service. Where there is a dispute the AMUSF will receive the customer's complaint in writing. The AMUSF sends the complaint to the member with the intention of encouraging the member to tell his side of the story. The AMUSF then tries to facilitate a resolution of the dispute based on a recommendation from the association or a compromise worked out between the parties by the association. The association refers to this process as 'mediation', although it can also be thought of as conciliation. However, where mediation fails, the customer may access the arbitration scheme. Full details of the process can be obtained by visiting www.upholsterers.co.uk.

Housing disrepair claims

There are various local authority complaints and/or arbitration procedures for tenants of local authorities. For example:

- In England the tenants of social landlords and some private landlords may take their complaints to The Independent Housing Ombudsman, 3rd Floor, Norman House, 105–109 The Strand, London WC2R 0AA. Tel: 020 7836 3630.

- In Wales, tenants may contact the National Assembly for Wales, Cathays Park, Cardiff CF10 3NQ. Tel: 029 2082 5111.

The Federation of Master Builders

The Federation of Master Builders (FMB) provides a dispute resolution process for the benefit of its members and their customers. Initially, a customer who is unhappy about a member's work may complete a complaint form. The regional office of the FMB then attempts to broker an agreement between member and customer. If that fails, then the FMB will appoint an independent third party to decide whether the complaint is justified. If it is, he will decide what steps should be taken to remedy the complaint. There is also an appeals process if either side is unhappy with the decision. For more details, visit www.fmb.org.uk.

Mediation

An independent neutral person, the mediator, assists the parties through individual meetings with him, as well as in joint sessions, to focus on their **real** interests and strengths as opposed to their emotions. The aim of the process is to draw the parties to a position where they set out their terms of settlement in a written document, which is legally enforceable.

Who are mediators?

A mediator is often, but not always, a lawyer. Mediators are generally trained and accredited by a mediation organisation to broker deals between potential or actual litigants. They are paid a fee by the parties. Paying the fees can be cheaper than court proceedings.

The mediator seeks to draw the parties together in the direction of possible settlement. Crucial to the mediation process is that the mediator ordinarily does not make recommendations as to what would be an appropriate settlement, but is merely there to assist the parties to find and settle their own agreement. However, it is a misconception to assume that the mediator is merely a sympathetic listener. He can be tough at times in giving direction to a party's thoughts during the individual and joint sessions.

Where are mediations held?

Until recently some County Courts operated their own mediation schemes and the mediations were held in court offices. Now the Department for Constitutional Affairs has introduced one scheme for mediation nationwide. This is the National Mediation Helpline. Mediations are sometimes held in other public buildings, such as church halls, community centres or even the home of one of the parties to the mediation. Usually it will boil down to the cheapest option where the claim is modest.

The advantages of mediation

- The process can be swift as a mediator is not affected by the court timetable.
- The process is private.
- The decisions are made by the parties rather than the District Judge.
- The details of what was said by the parties during the mediation cannot be revealed to the court should the mediation fail and court action be taken.

For further information visit <u>www.nationalmediationhelpline.com</u> or telephone 0845 603 0809, Monday to Friday from 08.30 to 18.00, where you will find details of the costs involved.

Alternatively, visit <u>www.talkmediation.co.uk</u> for a mediation scheme which has been recognised by the Civil Mediation Council. It is keen to promote resolution of smaller disputes. Write to them at Talk Mediation, 19–21 The Mews, King Street, Hereford HR4 9BX. Tel/Fax: 01432 267 832.

CHAPTER 3
Shaping your claim

Who do you sue?

It may seem obvious who the defendant to your claim is. However, the court rules require you to identify the defendant correctly, otherwise the claim cannot be validly pursued in the courts. If you begin your claim against Joseph Norris trading as 'Norris Nosh', when you actually made a contract with 'Norris Nosh (2004) Limited', Joseph Norris will be quite entitled to ask the court to strike out your claim. You would have to start the claim all over again and pay another fee to the court.

The categories of defendant are broadly the following:

Individuals

These are ordinary members of the public who are of sound mind and over 18 years of age. You can bring a claim against them in their own name. For example:

IN THE NORTHAMPTON COUNTY COURT   **Case No: 06/0001**

Claimant

Shoeler Accountancy Services (a partnership)

(Address including postcode)

> **Defendant**
>
> Rosie Smith
>
> (Address including postcode)

Sole traders

If your debtor is someone you are doing business with who is not a limited company, then he is a sole trader. For example, Rick Tailor who is an upholsterer and carries on business as 'Tailor's Upholstering' is a sole trader. He is not a limited company because he has never incorporated. You can bring a claim against him personally. This is what your Claim Form would look like:

> **IN THE NORTHAMPTON COUNTY COURT**   **Case No: 06/0002**
>
> **Claimant**
>
> Mary Broom
>
> (Address including postcode)
>
> **Defendant**
>
> Rick Tailor (sole trader, trading as 'Tailor's Upholstering')
>
> (Address including postcode)

Limited companies

A limited company is a business that has 'incorporated', which means that the directors of the company are not personally liable for any claim you bring against it. The company has what is called 'corporate personality' and so the company will pay a successful claim against it. This means that any claim against it must be brought against the company name and not against the directors of the company, unless the directors personally guaranteed any agreement.

Usually it is banks, building societies and finance providers that require personal guarantees from company directors. Some landlords require personal guarantees from the parents of university students signing tenancy agreements. However, whenever you sue a limited company you need to identify the company properly by giving its full name and address, including postcode, in the space on the Claim Form.

IN THE NORTHAMPTON COUNTY COURT   **Case No: 06/0003**

Claimant

Henry Whitley

(Address including postcode)

Defendant

Harwood Furniture Restoration Limited

Registered office: 27 Deans Road

Manchester M1 4GH

Partnerships

Partnerships are businesses in which the partners are personally liable for any claim against the partnership. However, the partnership does not have corporate personality and liability is unlimited. Each partner who is part of the partnership is liable to pay a judgment debt. This is called being 'jointly and severally' liable. If you are claiming against a partnership, the Claim Form will look like this:

IN THE NORTHAMPTON COUNTY COURT   **Case No: 06/0004**

Claimant

Ellen Jones

(Address including postcode)

Defendant

Shoeler Accountancy Services (a partnership)

Who carry on business at (address including postcode)

Limited liability partnerships (LLPs)

Some partnerships can be a limited liability partnership (LLP). So you would still bring the action in the name of the partnership but liability is not unlimited. The Claim Form would look like this:

> **IN THE NORTHAMPTON COUNTY COURT**   **Case No: 06/0005**
>
> **Claimant**
>
> Dean Kent
>
> (Address including postcode)
>
> **Defendant**
>
> Tompkins, Fulham and Co. LLP (a partnership)
>
> Who carry on business at (address including postcode)

Unincorporated associations

Most clubs and societies are unincorporated associations. This means that they are governed by a constitution (a set of rules) stating the purpose of the association and how it is organised and governed. If you wish to sue a club or society, you have to sue it through its officers because it has no 'legal personality' unlike a limited company. This means that the officers of the association are named as defendants on the Claim Form. Look at the examples below.

> **IN THE NORTHAMPTON COUNTY COURT**   **Case No: 06/0006**
>
> **Claimant**
>
> Terry Rawl
>
> (Address including postcode)
>
> **Defendant(s)**
>
> (1) George Scrubs (Chairman of and sued on behalf of the Bossingham Forest Association)
>
> (Address including postcode)
>
> (2) Henry Lawrence (Secretary of and sued on behalf of the Bossingham Forest Association)
>
> (Address including postcode)
>
> (3) Florence Hams (Treasurer of and sued on behalf of the Bossingham Forest Association)
>
> (Address including postcode)

If you win against the club or society, the officers will have to pay you from club funds. If there are insufficient club funds, they must personally pay the claim and then recover their losses from their members. Many clubs and societies carry public liability insurance in order to make provision for claims. If you are making a claim against a club or society, you should begin by writing to the club to ask for the name and address of the relevant insurance company and policy number, together with the full names and home addresses of the officers.

Children

Children can be sued in their own name, but they cannot act in litigation themselves. They need a 'next friend' to act for them. Look at the example below:

> Sam accidentally ran his bicycle into a car owned by Frank, a neighbour. Sam caused £300 worth of damage. Naturally, Frank spoke to Sam's father, who claimed Tim, not Sam, had caused the damage. Tim was with Sam at the time. Tim's father claimed that Sam had caused the damage. Frank decided to make a claim against both the children. He also adds their fathers to the claim for failing to supervise the boys adequately.

The top of the Claim Form looked like the one that follows:

IN THE NORTHAMPTON COUNTY COURT   **Case No: 06/0007**

Claimant

Frank Smith

(Address including postcode)

Defendant(s)

(1) Samuel Derby (a child, by Gregory Derby, his father and litigation friend)

(Address including postcode)

(2) Timothy Heggarty (a child, by Kenneth Heggarty, his father and litigation friend)

(Address including postcode)

> (3) Gregory Derby (father and litigation friend of first defendant)
>
> (Address including postcode)
>
> (4) Kenneth Heggarty (father and litigation friend of second defendant)
>
> (Address including postcode)

Frank gave a copy of the draft Claim Form to Mr Derby and Mr Heggarty, saying he would send them to the court in seven days. This was enough to persuade both fathers to pay for the damage to his car between them.

What do you claim?

Small claims generally concern claims for money. The aim is to obtain compensation. If you buy computer software that fails to do what it was supposed to do, then you will want to recover the cost of purchasing the software. However, the law will not give you compensation unless you have what is called 'a cause of action'. This means a legal ground for claiming compensation.

Look at the table on pages 45–8 to see what the law says about common complaints. These are breach of contract cases because there was a contract that has not been honoured by the service provider.

How long have I got to make the claim?

The law requires people who have a claim to bring it to the attention of the other side as soon as possible. The law does not regard it as fair for anyone to have a potential claim hanging over them for an indefinite period of time. As time goes on, memories fade and reliable evidence becomes less easy to retrieve. So the courts will not allow a claim to proceed unless it is made within a certain length of time. The earlier a claim is made the more reliable the evidence is likely to be.

If your claim is a contract claim, then you need to make your claim **within six years of the date the contract was breached**.

Some common breach of contract complaints

Facts	Contract – the law	What remedy/money can be claimed
Your mobile phone only works intermittently. The phone company's salesman gave you a contract with a finance company to sign, which stated that the agreement would run for three years. The sales agent said that you could cancel the agreement after two years. This is the only reason why you were prepared to sign it for three years! The finance company states that you must pay a penalty of £600 for cancelling early and all the rentals for the last 12 months of the agreement.	Breach of implied terms of the agreement under section 14 of the Sale of Goods Act 1979, as amended by the Sale and Supply of Goods Act 1994. This is because the phone was not of 'satisfactory' quality. The salesman was the agent of the finance company with whom the agreement was made. Breach of warranty that the agreement could be terminated after two years. Penalty clause unfair within the meaning of the Unfair Contracts Terms Act 1977 and the Unfair Terms in Consumer Contracts Regulations 1999.	Declaration that the penalty clause is unfair and should be struck down. Compensation for failure to provide a mobile phone that works adequately.
A 'pre-owned' car turns out to be a wreck.	Breach of implied terms of contract pursuant to sections 13 and 14 of the Sale of Goods Act 1979, as amended by the Sale and Supply of Goods Act 1994 that the car would be of satisfactory	'Rescission' of the sale agreement and all the money paid back. This remedy is only available if it is claimed quickly and

Some common breach of contract complaints (continued)

Facts	Contract – the law	What remedy/money can be claimed
	quality for a car of its age and type and fit for the purpose of being driven.	the car is returned to the seller. Consumers are more likely to end up with money compensation for the losses suffered. This is the difference between what was paid for the car and its actual market value, in the condition in which it was supplied.
A small business purchases a new computer to keep the accounts, PAYE records for five employees and the book-keeping ledgers and correspondence. The computer software does not work as it should and the computer keeps crashing. The book-keeper has to spend time sorting it out.	Breach of implied terms that the software would be of satisfactory quality and fit for its purpose, pursuant to sections 13 and 14 of the Sale of Goods Act 1979, as amended by the Sale and Supply of Goods Act 1994.	The cost of the software and the cost of taking time to take the computer to the computer repair shop to remove the software and data and reload the old software and data.

Some common breach of contract complaints (continued)

Facts	Contract – the law	What remedy/money can be claimed
A builder installs a new kitchen that costs £11,000. After the installation is complete, the householder notices that:		
1. the door of the 'built-in' refrigerator does not fit properly because it juts out from the line of the rest of the kitchen cupboard units;	Breach of implied terms that the kitchen would be of satisfactory quality and fit for its purpose, pursuant to sections 13 and 14 of the Sale of Goods Act 1979, as amended by the Sale and Supply of Goods Act 1994.	The cost of replacing the failed kitchen appliances. The cost of replacing the unit that does not match the others. The cost of engaging a kitchen fitter to take out the failed items and install new ones.
2. the extractor fan does not work because the unit is broken;	Breach of implied term of the contract to carry out the work with due care and skill by section 13 of the Supply of Goods and Services Act 1982, as amended by the Sale and Supply of Goods Act 1994.	Compensation for vexation and inconvenience of the kitchen breakdown.
3. one of the wall cupboard doors does not match the colour of the rest of the units;	Breach of section 4(2) of the Supply of Goods and Services Act 1982 in that the appliances supplied were not of satisfactory quality.	
4. the seal on the sink leaks, the freezer ices up very quickly and when it does the door will not shut;		
5. one of the two plinth heaters has failed.		

Some common breach of contract complaints (continued)

Facts	Contract – the law	What remedy/money can be claimed
A motor car is taken to a garage to be repaired. When the owner collects it he notices that the hub caps are missing and the satellite navigation system has been removed. The garage insists that it was locked up while it was with them and will not pay for the missing items.	Breach of 'bailment'. The garage was under a duty to look after the vehicle while it was being repaired and to ensure that it was locked away securely when unattended. Negligent omission to ensure that the premises was secure against theft.	The cost of replacing the hub caps and the satellite navigation system.
Three-piece suite reupholstering poorly executed. Fabric sagging on the cushions and the piping on the cushions does not line up properly with the piping on the back cushions of the sofa.	Breach of implied term of the contract to carry out the work with due care and skill by section 13 of the Supply of Goods and Services Act 1982, as amended by the Sale and Supply of Goods Act 1994.	The cost of labour and materials wasted in having the work carried out properly.

Here is an example of how the rule works:

Laura engaged Rick to reupholster her three-piece suite of furniture in October 2005. In March 2006 she noticed that the cushions were sagging and contacted Rick. Rick said that there was nothing wrong with his work and that it was a natural consequence of using a natural filling.

Laura continued to write to and telephone Rick for the next four months, but he still maintained that there was nothing wrong with his work. Laura then began a claim against Rick in the Small Claims Court. When Laura received his defence it stated that under his terms and conditions she was only entitled to complain within seven days of the date of delivery of the furniture. Rick, who was represented by a lawyer, asked the court to strike out her claim.

The court did not strike out Laura's claim. The District Judge stated that Laura was entitled to bring her claim within six years of October 2005 and that she was entitled to question the fairness of the clause in Rick's contract.

Contrast this with another case:

Darren is a lecturer at the University of Felthon. He ordered a review copy of a book that he recommended to his students on 4 April 2000. The publisher's terms and conditions of sale therefore entitled him to a free copy.

Three years later, in December 2003, he received a final demand letter from the publisher threatening to sue him if he did not pay for the book. Darren immediately emailed the publisher a copy of the recommendation he had given to his students in April 2000. Then Darren heard no more about it until May 2006 when he received yet another demand letter and a threat to sue him.

Darren was unable to send a further copy of his last email because the university's computer system had been changed and it had not been saved on the old back-up records. When he received a Claim Form from the court he wrote and asked the court to strike out the claim on the ground that the publisher had to bring its claim within six years. The District Judge agreed and struck out the publisher's claim.

There is an exception to this rule. If your claim concerns a contract which was made 'under seal' (e.g. a contract for the sale or purchase of land or one signed as a 'deed'), then you may bring your claim within 12 years of the breach occurring. If you are not sure whether the contract was under seal, you should seek professional legal advice.

Other types of civil wrongs

Generally a claim for any other type of civil wrong (called a 'tort') must be made usually **within six years of the damage occurring which is caused by the wrongful or negligent act or omission**. However, if the wrong is a **personal injury**, the claim must be brought **within three years of the date of injury, or the date of knowledge of the injury**. If you are not clear about when the injury occurred, you may need to take specialist legal advice about that matter.

On pages 51–2 are some examples of claims where the law involved is not about breach of contract. They are other civil wrongs.

Working out the date of breach in a personal injury

Here is an illustration of how it can work. Let's look further at the story of Raj's accident referred to on page 52.

The accident occurred on 18 February. At first, Raj believed that he had suffered no physical injuries, but after a week (i.e. 25 February) he began to get persistent headaches and then to suffer neck pain. A visit to the doctor confirmed that he had suffered a whiplash injury. Therefore, Raj needs to make his claim for his personal injuries within three years of the date of discovering he was physically injured, i.e. 25 February.

Here is a more complicated example:

In 1993, when Sharon was 16 years old, she liked to go to all-night

Some common 'civil wrong' complaints

Facts	Law	Remedy/money claim
John has a mongrel dog called Leo. One day the dog escaped from his house and went to Katie's house. Katie's female dog, Lulu, was in the front seat of her car. Leo was very fond of Lulu and jumped up and down making lots of scratches to the paint of Katie's 'pearl' pink car. The cost of repairing the paint is £500.	Negligent omission to keep Leo securely indoors. John should have ensured that Leo did not escape and cause damage to Katie's car.	The cost of respraying the door of Katie's car.
Elsie twisted her ankle and bruised both knees in her local high street when she tripped over a loose flagstone. Her injuries took six months to heal and settle.	Negligent omission by the highway authority to ensure that the pavement was repaired properly.	Compensation for her pain, suffering and expenses, which were taxi fares to the doctor, taxi fares to the hospital for physiotherapy for the sprained ankle, prescription charges and mobile telephone calls.

Some common 'civil wrong' complaints (continued)

Facts	Law	Remedy/money claim
Doreen lives about 300 yards away from a neighbouring farm where a farmer breeds and rears wild boar. One afternoon the boars escaped and went into Doreen's garden where they ate all her plants and flowers, and dug up her vegetables.	Negligence and trespass to property. Section 4(1) of the Animals Act 1971.	The cost of replacing the plants and garden produce.
Raj is driving his car on an afternoon when the roads are almost empty. He slows down as he nears the traffic lights, but a green car behind him fails to stop in sufficient time and crashes into the rear of his car once he is stationary. His laptop computer was in the rear of the car and was irreparably damaged.	Negligence.	The cost of repairing the extensive damage to his car. Compensation for the time he had to take off work to get his car removed and to contact his insurers, and the cost of his mobile telephone calls. The cost of replacing his laptop computer.

discos and clubs with her friends. They went regularly to the 'Buzz Buzz Nightclub' every Thursday and Friday night for nearly five years. The music at the club was very loud and some of her friends wouldn't go because it was so loud.

Sharon gave birth to her first child two years ago. In October 2005, when she was 28 years old, she found herself turning up the volume on the television and the radio. Sometimes she cannot hear everything her daughter is saying to her. When Sharon's doctor sent her to the hospital for tests in December 2005 she discovered that she had suffered permanent hearing loss in her right ear. The hospital consultant considered the cause is most likely to be the noise to which she was exposed by the nightclub disco. When she wrote to the club it denied it was at fault and stated that she had consented to exposure to the noise. The club also said that she was out of time to make any claim.

Sharon's personal injury claim arises from the date of discovery of the injury which is the time **at which she discovered she was not hearing as well** as she once did, i.e. October 2005. Therefore, Sharon needs to make her claim within three years of October 2005.

Where do I start?

You need to identify the court in which you will start your claim. One way of finding out which court deals with claims where you live or carry on business is to visit www.hmcourts-service.gov.uk. Follow the links to the list of County Courts for your region. Another way is to look up your telephone directory where all your local County Courts are listed.

The 'letter before action'

If you have not already warned your debtor that you will take legal action should he fail to satisfy your claim, you should do so without delay. Take note of Brian and Carol's letter before action on the following page.

Example claim letter 6

**Brian & Carol Clarke, Sheiling Lawn Cottage,
Bays Lane, Oxon OX9 3PP**

George Biddulph
Claybourne Building Services Ltd
Walnut Copse
Peerpoint Housing Estate
Oxon OX5 6YY

6 April 2006

Dear Mr Biddulph,

Re: Our conservatory

1. We regret that despite several telephone calls from us, you have failed to put right the defects to our conservatory.

2. We attach the bill we received from the builder we were forced to engage to put right your shoddy work.

3. Unless within seven days of the date of this letter you make full payment to us of £1,192.63, together with interest at the rate of eight per cent, plus our out-of-pocket expenses on telephone calls, we shall make a claim in the County Court.

4. We urge you to settle our claim because we shall be calling the builder who put your work right to give evidence at court. We shall have to pay his expenses and we shall ask the court to order you to pay them when we win.

Yours sincerely,

Brian & Carol Clarke

The Civil Procedure Rules

Everything that happens in the civil courts is governed by a set of rules called The Civil Procedure Rules 1998 (CPR). These rules determine how the court operates. This single set of rules covers both High and County Courts.

This book is aimed at explaining the law and procedures of the Small Claims Court simply, so it does not set out the legal rules. However, there is one rule you should know about. It is called the 'overriding objective'. It is the most important rule in the CPR because the court must give effect to the overriding objective whenever it exercises any power under the rules.

Rule 1 sets out the overriding objective:

1.1 (1) These Rules are a new procedural code with the overriding objective of enabling the court to deal with cases justly.

(2) Dealing with a case justly includes, so far as is practicable –

(a) ensuring that the parties are on an equal footing;

(b) saving expense;

(c) dealing with the case in ways which are proportionate –

(i) to the amount of money involved;

(ii) to the importance of the case;

(iii) to the complexity of the issues; and

(iv) to the financial position of each party;

(d) ensuring that it is dealt with expeditiously and fairly; and

(e) allotting to it an appropriate share of the court's resources, while taking into account the need to allot resources to other cases.

The CPR are available at www.dca.gov.uk/procedurerules.htm.

This rule means that District Judges must do what they can to ensure that small claims do not become complex or involve needless expense. So when the District Judge sees the claim documents before the trial he will be considering how best to **settle** the dispute, not just how to **decide** the dispute.

CHAPTER 4

Getting the ball rolling

Accessing the forms

There are several ways of doing this:

- Go to your local County Court and pick up the forms from the court office.

- Go to The Stationery Office (TSO) and purchase forms there.

- Use Lawpack's *Small Claims Kit* (www.lawpack.co.uk).

- Use Money Claim Online to start your claim – this will be discussed in detail later.

- Visit www.hmcourts-service.gov.uk to download the forms. Pick up free information leaflets EX301 and EX302 about making a claim. For small businesses there is leaflet EX350, which includes a very helpful flow chart.

- Visit www.hmcourts-service.gov.uk/countycourtformsonline, where you can complete the court forms online and transmit them electronically to those courts that are participating in the pilot scheme that is testing the process. If it is successful, then it is likely to be extended to other courts. A list of the participating courts can be found at the address above.

Whichever route you choose, you will end up having to complete a Claim Form called the N1. The N1 sets out the details of your claim. The court will not serve the N1 on the defendant unless it is completed properly. The N1 Form is accompanied by two pages of notes (N1A) to assist the user. You need to read this form before you start to complete the N1.

As the form is available online, you may choose to complete it electronically and then print it off. You will have the advantage of being able to print off the exact number of copies you need. If you are completing the form by hand, you should complete it in black ink because the court requires you to do so and also because you will need to photocopy the form. Whether you type or handwrite your N1, you will need the following copies:

- The original N1
- One copy for each defendant
- One copy of the N1, for your own file

Completing the form

The court

The first box to be filled in is the box in the top right-hand corner. You will find 'In the…' written there. This is the part where you type the court in which you are bringing the claim. It is best to use capital letters here.

The claimant

Then go down to the heading 'Claimant'. Write or type in your name and address, including the postcode. If you do not know the postcode, visit www.royalmail.com where this information can be obtained free. If you do not include the postcode, the court will not serve the Claim Form on the defendant.

The defendant

Under the heading 'Defendant', type or write the name and address of the defendant, including the postcode. You must insert the defendant's full name where it is known. This is because it will help the court to identify the defendant correctly if you do have to enforce a judgment. If you are claiming against a limited company, remember to put the registered office address of the company or the address at which it carries on business.

Brief details of the claim

The details should be as brief as you can make them. Further details can be written in a section on the second page of the N1. So if you are claiming the cost of an unpaid bill or invoice, you can put 'Unpaid invoice' and then add 'See attached copy', and put a copy of the bill at the back of the N1 Form.

Here are some alternatives, although they are not the only ones you can use.

Examples of brief details of claim

- Unpaid bill/invoice/fees
- Physical injury to claimant
- Delivery of damaged goods
- Damage to claimant's property
- Physical injury to claimant and damage to claimant's property
- Hire purchase contract dispute
- Cost of putting right defective work to claimant's property by defendant
- Unpaid rent
- Claim against landlord for disrepair/return of deposit
- Holiday claim

Statement of value

Simply fill in the money value of your claim under the word 'Value'. Brian and Carol are claiming £1,192.63 as the cost of putting right the defective work on their conservatory.

There may be times when you cannot precisely know what figure to put upon your claim; for example, if your claim is for physical injury, put in 'Up to £1,000'. If your personal injury claim is worth more than £1,000, the court will transfer it to another track. Many small personal injury claims are combined with claims for damage to property. The total sum you claim, excluding accrued contractual interest, must still be below £5,000 if you wish to remain in the Small Claims Court. If you are unsure what the court will award for other small claims (e.g. noise nuisance), then claim 'Up to £5,000'. Do not omit to put in a figure because the court will not issue your Claim Form otherwise.

The Human Rights Act 1998

If you suspect that your claim concerns any issue under the Human Rights Act, you need to consult a lawyer. Otherwise simply tick the 'No' box on the form.

Particulars of Claim

This is the part of the Claim Form where you should set out your claim more fully. This really means just explaining to the court why you are entitled to make your claim. Here are some examples of Particulars of Claim you could use, if appropriate:

Brief details of claim	Particulars of Claim examples
Unpaid bill/invoice/fees	The claimant claims the sum of £[insert amount] due from the defendant to the claimant under an unpaid invoice/bill/fee note dated [insert date] for goods/services supplied by the claimant to the

	defendant. A copy of the unpaid invoice/bill/fee note(s) is/are attached to this Claim Form.
Physical injury to claimant	The claimant claims up to £5,000 for personal injuries sustained by the claimant while a lawful visitor to the defendant's premises on [insert date]. By reason of the defendant's negligence, and/or breach of duty of care, the claimant suffered a sprained ankle, cuts and bruises that required hospital treatment and caused him pain, suffering and financial loss. A copy of the claimant's hospital/General Practitioner's notes are attached to this Claim Form. A schedule of the claimant's special damages is attached to this Claim Form.
Delivery of damaged goods	The claimant claims the sum of £[insert amount], being the sum paid by the claimant to the defendant for goods supplied to the claimant by the defendant but which were damaged and/or of unsatisfactory quality and/or not fit for the purpose at the point of delivery to the claimant. The claimant brought this to the attention of the defendant by email/fax/letter/telephone call on [insert date], but the defendant has wrongfully, and in breach of the agreement between itself and the claimant, failed to supply credit for the damaged goods or substitute goods of satisfactory quality, fit for the purpose for which the goods were sold.

Damage to claimant's property	By reason of the defendant's negligence and/or breach of duty of care the claimant suffered financial loss when the defendant's dog, a 'golden retriever' wearing an identification tag, escaped from the defendant's house and jumped up at the front passenger-seat door of the claimant's pink Vauxhall Vectra, registration number AK05 DFG. The defendant's dog scratched the paint on the front passenger-seat door and the repair will cost the claimant £500. Despite the claimant requesting payment of the repair cost by a letter dated [insert date], the defendant has wrongfully failed to make payment to the claimant.
Physical injury to claimant and damage to claimant's property	The claimant claims the sum of £1,000 for a whiplash injury he sustained on [insert date] when the defendant negligently drove his BMW estate car, registration number CK03 6TY, into the claimant's stationary Fiat Uno car, registration number JK04 9NM, at the traffic lights at Oakfield Road, Ashton-under-Lyne, Lancashire, at its junction with Manchester Road. The claimant further claims £2,000 for damage caused to his vehicle by the negligence of the defendant and the claimant attaches his medical reports and garage repair bills to this Claim Form.
Claim for return of tenant's deposit	The claimant is a tenant of the defendant under an agreement pursuant to [insert relevant statute] dated for a period of [insert time

period]. A copy of the agreement is attached to the Claim Form. By clause [*insert clause number in agreement*], the claimant made payment of a deposit of £[*insert amount*] on [*insert date*]. The deposit was equivalent to one month's rent. On the expiry of the tenancy, and by letter dated [*insert date*], the claimant requested the return of the deposit in accordance with the agreement. Wrongfully and in breach of the agreement the defendant has failed to return the deposit. The claimant therefore claims the return of the deposit in the sum of £[*insert amount*], together with interest.

Unpaid rent	The claimant is the defendant's landlord. Under an agreement regulated by [*insert the Housing or property Act that applies to the tenancy*] and dated [*insert date*] the defendant was obliged to pay rent of £[*insert amount*] on each [*insert day*] of the month for a period of [*insert length of tenancy*]. In breach of the agreement, (attached to this Claim Form), the defendant failed to make rent payments on [*insert dates*] causing the claimant loss. Under the terms of the agreement the claimant notified the defendant of his failure by letter dated [*insert date*] (attached to Claim Form), but the defendant has failed to pay the sums due to the claimant. Therefore the claimant claims the unpaid rents of £[*insert figure*], together with interest.

Claim against landlord for disrepair	The claimant is a tenant of the defendant under an agreement regulated by [*insert the Housing or property Act that applies to the tenancy*] and dated [*insert date*]. Under clause [*insert clause in agreement*] of the agreement the defendant was obliged to keep the rented property occupied by the claimant fit for habitation and in reasonable repair and condition. By letter dated [*insert date*], a copy of which is attached to this Claim Form, the claimant notified the defendant that a leaky pipe in the roof space above the bathroom had caused the ceiling to sag. Water ingress and debris from the sagging ceiling prevented the claimant from using the bathroom. Despite the claimant notifying him, the defendant failed to make a proper repair. The claimant was forced to employ a builder to repair the leak, take down the old 'plaster and lath' ceiling, replace it with plaster board and then apply 'Artex' and repaint the new ceiling at a cost of £850. The claimant claims £850, together with damages for distress, vexation, inconvenience and interest, limited to £1,000. The claimant attaches photographs of the disrepair and copy bills verifying his claim to this Claim Form.

Claiming interest

After the 'Particulars of Claim' you need another paragraph below this section for claiming interest payments. All County Court judgments for money payments attract interest at the rate of eight per cent per annum from the date the sum became due to the date of the judgment. This is because the law aims to compensate claimants who have been unjustly kept out of payment of the sums due to them at an earlier date. The interest payments you are claiming should be calculated from the date the money became due to the date of issue of the claim by the court and then a daily rate of interest claimed from the date of issue of the claim. Let's see how the interest should be claimed in Brian and Carol's case:

Brian and Carol are claiming £1,192.63, which became due to 4Walls Maintenance Company Ltd on 2 February 2006. Therefore, they may claim interest from 2 February to the date of issue of their Claim Form on 13 April 2006.

Brian and Carol need to start by working out the annual interest on the sum they are claiming.

£1,192.63 x 8(%) = 9,541.04

9,541.04 ÷ 100 − 95.41

To work out the daily rate of interest:

95.41 ÷ 365 days = 26 pence per day

There are 70 days between 2 February 2006 and the date of issue of the Claim Form on 13 April 2006.

70 x 26 pence = £18.20 to the date of issue.

Brian and Carol must claim interest of £18.20 and 26 pence per day after that until the date of judgment or payment, whichever is sooner.

Sometimes a contract states that a claimant who has suffered late payment can claim contractual interest. This is often expressed as 'x% over base for the time being of XYZ Bank Plc'. Also, businesses should consider claiming interest under the Late Payment of Commercial Debts (Interest) Act 1999. Visit www.payontime.co.uk.

Look at the second page of Brian and Carol's N1 Form to see how the interest paragraph is set out.

Example Claim Form N1

Claim Form	**In the**	SWINDON COUNTY COURT
		for court use only
	Claim No.	SW
Click here to clear your data after printing	Issue date	13 April 2006

SEAL

Claimant

(1) Brian Clarke
(2) Carol Clarke

Defendant(s)

Claybourne Building Services Ltd

Brief details of claim

Cost of putting right defective work carried out under contract made in October 2005.

Value

£1,192.63

Defendant's name and address		£	
Claybourne Building Services Ltd Walnut Copse Peerpoint Housing Estate OXON OX5 6YY	Amount claimed	1,192.63
	Court fee	120.00
	Solicitor's costs	
	Total amount	1,312.63

The court office at

is open between 10 am and 4 pm Monday to Friday. When corresponding with the court, please address forms or letters to the Court Manager and quote the claim number.

N1 Claim form (CPR Part 7) (01.02)   *Printed on behalf of The Court Service*

Example Claim Form N1 (continued)

Claim No.	SW

Does, or will, your claim include any issues under the Human Rights Act 1998? ☑ Yes ☐ No

Particulars of Claim (attached)(to follow)

The claimant and the defendant made a contract in October 2005 in accordance with the defendant's estimate dated 11 October 2005. The claimant paid 50 per cent of the contract price before work began and the balance on completion on 18 November 2005.

In breach of the contract, the defendant failed to carry out the agreed work competently and failed to supply window and door handles that matched or were fit for their purpose or of satisfactory quality. As a result, the claimant was forced to engage another builder to put right the defendant's work. The defects are set out in the attached bill from 4Walls Maintenance Company Ltd dated 2 February 2006.

Despite the claimant's letter before action of 6 April 2006, which is attached to this Claim Form, the defendant has refused to make payment of the cost of putting the work right in the sum of £1,192.63 and is liable to pay damages to the claimant with interest.

The claimant claims £1,192.63, together with interest pursuant to section 69 of the County Courts Act 1984, at the rate of eight per cent per annum from 2 February 2006 to the date of issue of £18.20, and continuing at the daily rate of £0.26 to the date of judgment or payment, whichever is the sooner.

Statement of Truth
*(I believe)(The Claimant believes) that the facts stated in these particulars of claim are true.
* I am duly authorised by the claimant to sign this statement

Full name *Brian Clarke*   *Carol Clarke*

Name of claimant's solicitor's firm _____

signed _____   position or office held _____
*(Claimant)(Litigation friend)(Claimant's solicitor)   (if signing on behalf of firm or company)
*delete as appropriate

Claimant's or claimant's solicitor's address to which documents or payments should be sent if different from overleaf including (if appropriate) details of DX, fax or e-mail.

Statement of truth

In this section you need to strike out the appropriate words. The statement of truth is a very important part of the Claim Form. It is a certificate that the contents of your claim document are true. If it is not signed, the court may not permit you to rely upon the contents of the Claim Form as evidence of your case. So it is easier to ensure that you sign the statement of truth.

Disability issues

If, for any reason, you cannot physically sign the statement of truth or cannot read it, then you will need to find an 'authorised person' to help you. An authorised person is someone who is permitted by law to administer oaths, such as a Notary Public or a solicitor. You simply put the following writing on the Claim Form:

'I certify that I [*full name and address of the authorised person*] have read over the contents of this document and the statement of truth to the person signing the document, [*and explained the nature and effect of the exhibits referred to in it*], who appeared to understand (a) the document and approved its contents as accurate; and (b) the declaration of truth and the consequences of making a false declaration and made his mark in my presence.'

Then find an authorised person to formally read the documents to you. Most high-street solicitors are quite willing to help with this. Simply ask if they have any one who can swear affidavits or administer oaths. Remember to ask what they charge for this service too.

Address for documents

The same rules apply here as before. The address should be the full address and include the postcode. If you are willing to accept the service of documents by fax or email, you should insert those details.

Issuing the claim

The process by which your claim becomes a proceeding of the court is called 'issuing' the claim. This means that the court receives your Claim Form in person or by post, email or electronically via Money Claim Online (MCOL) and then a court administrator gives your claim a claim number and an issue date. The claim number and issue date are inserted into the spaces on the right-hand corner of the Claim Form. The court will only issue the claim when:

- the statement of value is complete;

- the statement of truth is signed;

- the Claim Form is complete and is accompanied by the correct court fee; and

- the right number of copies have been provided for service on the defendant(s).

If you intend dealing with the court by post, it is a good idea to send the court a covering letter with your Claim Form. It will help you to see that you have done all you need to do and it will be a record of your request to the court. On the following page is an example covering letter that Brian and Carol used. In this case, Carol has a friend who works in a solicitor's office and she advised Carol to write the letter.

If the court is satisfied that the claim may be issued, it will:

- stamp the court seal on the original Claim Form you have signed with the statement of truth;

- stamp the copy Claim Forms for your records;

- stamp one copy of the Claim Form for each defendant who is being served with the Claim Form;

- write or stamp the issue date onto the original Claim Form and all the copies.

The court calls stamping the Claim Forms 'sealing'. The copies it stamps are called 'sealed' copies. The court then retains the original Claim Form

Carol's covering letter to the court

Brian & Carol Clarke, Sheiling Lawn Cottage, Bays Lane, Oxon OX9 3PP

Swindon County Court
The Law Courts
Islington Street
Swindon
Wiltshire SN1 2HG

13 April 2006

Dear Sir,

We enclose:

1.   Original Claim Form for court records

2.   Two copies of the Claim Form

3.   Issue fee of £120

Please return one sealed copy to us for our files and arrange service by post on the defendant. The address appears on the Claim Form.

Yours faithfully,

Brian & Carol Clarke

Enc.

for its file and returns a sealed copy Claim Form to you. Unless you tell the court that you will serve the defendant, it will send a sealed Claim Form to each defendant. The court will notify you that it has issued the Claim Form by sending you a Notice of Issue of Claim Form called N205A. The most important information it contains is the issue date and the claim number. Whenever you telephone the court, you **must quote the claim number**. When you write to the court you need to write the claim number on your letters or the court will not be able to locate your file quickly.

Serving the Claim Form

When the Claim Form has been issued, the defendant must receive notice of the claim against him. This process is called 'service' of the claim. There are several methods for serving court documents in England and Wales. But the following are the most usual:

- Court service by first-class post
- Personal service
- Service by fax

Court service

The court serves the Claim Form by first-class post. The date of service of the Claim Form is deemed to be the second day after it was posted. This becomes important because the defendant must respond to the claim within 14 days of the date of service of the Claim Form. If the court sends a Claim Form by first-class post on Thursday 16 March 2006, then the date of service will be Saturday 18 March 2006. When the court serves the Claim Form it will send you a Notice of Service of Issue Form N205A stating the date of issue and the deemed date of service.

Personal service

This type of service means that the Claim Form is personally delivered to the defendant. This type of service is used where the defendant is trying to avoid service. Unless you are faced with this problem, it is best to let the court serve the Claim Form. Usually a person called a 'process server' delivers the Claim Form to the defendant. In order to prove that the Claim Form was served, the process server will complete an N215 Form called a Certificate of Service Form. The details on the form simply record and verify how personal service was carried out. An example of Form N215 can be found on the following page.

The deemed date of service for this method is the moment of service, provided it is a working day and before 5pm. If service takes place after 5pm on a bank holiday or on Saturday or Sunday, service is deemed to be the next business day (i.e. any day other than Saturday, Sunday or a bank holiday).

Service by fax or email

The court rules do allow defendants to be served by fax or email by claimants. However, your debtor or the defendant must inform you in writing that he is willing to be served electronically. Furthermore, the court rules oblige you to ask the debtor what format he requires and the maximum size of attachments he can receive. Where service is by electronic means, the deemed date of service is the second day after the day of transmission.

Responding to the Claim Form

When the court serves the defendant, your Claim Form is not the only document he receives. When the defendant opens the letter from the court he will find a 'Response Pack'. These are the documents that permit the defendant to respond to your claim. For claims for specific amounts of money, they are as follows:

- Claim Form N1 and N1A notes
- Form N9
- Form N9A
- Form N1C

Example Certificate of Service Form N215

Certificate of service

Name of court	Claim No.
Name of Claimant	
Name of Defendant	

On the ....(insert date)

the .... (insert title or description of documents served)

a copy of which is attached to this notice was served on (insert name of person served, including position i.e. partner, director if appropriate)

....

Tick as appropriate

- [ ] by first class post or (with effect from 6th April 2006) an alternative service which provides for delivery on the next working day
- [ ] by Document Exchange

- [ ] by delivering to or leaving at a permitted place (see notes overleaf)
- [ ] by personally handing it to or leaving it with (please specify)

- [ ] by fax machine (....................time sent) (you may want to enclose a copy of the transmission sheet)
- [ ] by other electronic means (please specify)

- [ ] by other means permitted by the court (please specify)

at (insert address where service effected, include fax or DX number e-mail address or other electronic identification)

being the [ ] claimant's   [ ] defendant's   [ ] solicitor's   [ ] litigation friend:

- [ ] usual residence
- [ ] last known residence
- [ ] place of business
- [ ] principal place of business
- [ ] last known place of business

- [ ] principal office of the corporation
- [ ] principal office of the company
- [ ] other (please specify)

The date of service is therefore deemed to be .... (insert date - see overleaf for guidance)

I believe that the facts stated in this Certificate are true.

Full name

Signed
(Claimant)(Defendant)('s solicitor)('s litigation friend)

Position or office held
(if signing on behalf of firm or company)

Date

N215 Certificate of service (01.06)

HMCS

- Form N9B

They are as follows for claims for unspecific amounts of money or other remedies.

- Claim Form N1
- Form N9
- Form N9(C)
- Form N9D

Form N9 – Acknowledgment of Service

This is called the Acknowledgment of Service Form. The defendant must complete the form and return it to the court to show that he is aware of the claim. This applies whether the claim is for a specified amount or not. The defendant must do so **within 14 days** of the date of service of the Claim Form. An example of the form, completed by George Biddulph, can be found on the following page.

The top of the form tells the defendant what documents he has received and that he should read the 'notes for defendant' attached to the Claim Form. The instructions on the Response Pack also explain which documents the defendant must complete. The instructions make it clear that failing to respond is not an option for the defendant because of the consequences.

You can see from the example Acknowledgment of Service Form that the defendant has the following choices:

- Ignore the claim
- Admit the claim and/or ask for time to pay
- Admit part of the claim
- Dispute the whole of the claim or make a 'counterclaim' against the defendant
- Dispute the power of the court to hear the case

Example Acknowledgment of Service Form N9

Response Pack

You should read the 'notes for defendant' attached to the claim form which will tell you when and where to send the forms

Included in this pack are:

* either **Admission Form N9A**
  (if the claim is for a specified amount)
  or **Admission Form N9C**
  (if the claim is for an unspecified amount
  or is not a claim for money)

* either **Defence and Counterclaim Form**
  N9B (if the claim is for a specified amount)
  or **Defence and Counterclaim Form N9D**
  (if the claim is for an unspecified amount
  or is not a claim for money)

* **Acknowledgment of service**
  (see below)

Complete

If you admit the claim or the amount claimed and/or you want time to pay ►	the admission form
If you admit part of the claim ►	the admission form and the defence form
If you dispute the whole claim or wish to make a claim (a counterclaim) against the claimant ►	the defence form
If you need 28 days (rather than 14) from the date of service to prepare your defence, or wish to contest the court's jurisdiction ►	the acknowledgment of service
If you do nothing, judgment may be entered against you	

Acknowledgment of Service

Defendant's full name if different from the name given on the claim form

In the	SWINDON COUNTY COURT
Claim No.	SW065768
Claimant (including ref.)	Brian Clarke Carol Clarke
Defendant	Claybourne Building Services Ltd

Address to which documents about this claim should be sent (including reference if appropriate)

Claybourne Building Services Ltd
Walnut Copse
Peerpoint Housing Estate
OXON

Tel. no.   Postcode OX5 6YY

	if applicable
fax no.	01632 455 666
DX no.	
Ref. no.	
e-mail	Mail@claybourne

Tick the appropriate box

1. I intend to defend all of this claim ☑

2. I intend to defend part of this claim ☐

3. I intend to contest jurisdiction ☐

(My) (Defendant's) date of birth is `0 9 0 7 1 9 6 5`

If you file an acknowledgment of service but do not file a defence within 28 days of the date of service of the claim form, or particulars of claim if served separately, judgment may be entered against you.

If you do not file an application to dispute the jurisdiction of the court within 14 days of the date of filing this acknowledgment of service, it will be assumed that you accept the court's jurisdiction and judgment may be entered against you.

Signed *George Biddulph*

(Defendant)(Defendant's solicitor)(Litigation friend)

Position or office held Managing Director

(if signing on behalf of firm or company)

24 April 2006

Date

The court office at

is open between 10 am and 4 pm Monday to Friday. When corresponding with the court, please address forms or letters to the Court Manager and quote the claim number.

N9 Response Pack (04.06)

HMCS

You can see that George Biddulph has denied Brian and Carol's claim by ticking box 1. Brian and Carol find out when the court sends them sealed copies of the Acknowledgment of Service Form and Defence.

The debtor fails to reply to your claim

George Biddulph responded promptly to Brian and Carol's claim, which was a wise move. If he had not replied to the claim, then Brian and Carol could have entered judgment against him in default of acknowledgment of service.

If your debtor fails to respond within 14 days of service of the Claim Form, you can enter judgment. The court will not do it for you. You have to apply to the court for judgment in default of acknowledgment of service by completing Form N205A. If your debtor acknowledges service of the claim but does not file a defence with the court, you can enter judgment in default of service of a defence. Complete Form N205A.

Once the N205A Form is completed you need to make a copy for your file and one for each defendant and send it to the court. No fee is payable for this. When the court receives Form N205A it seals the original and the copy forms and returns one copy to you and the other to the defendant. The court then enters judgment against the defendant and enters his name on the court's register of judgment debtors.

The debtor admits all of your claim

A Claim Form from the County Court can be all that is needed to get the debtor to pay up. You will know if the debtor has accepted your claim because the court will send you a sealed copy of the admission form the defendant sent to the court. The defendant will have ticked the box stating 'I admit the full amount claimed as shown on the Claim Form'. At that stage many debtors simply send a cheque for the full sum, including the Claim Form issue fee and any interest that is owed on the debt. If this happens, you will need to inform the court.

Sometimes a debtor faced with court proceedings attempts to pay the debt but does not pay the interest and issue fee for the Claim Form. If your debtor does this, then bank the cheque 'on account of the full sum owed', inform the court and then tell your debtor that you will proceed with the claim and enter judgment on the remaining costs and interest unless they too are paid. The court will not do this automatically. You will need to complete Form N205A Request for Judgment (Specified Amount) or Form 205B (Unspecified Amount). It is important to complete the form correctly to show the sum you are claiming, the interest that has accumulated since the Claim Form was issued and any costs shown on the Claim Form. An example of Form N205A can be found on the following page.

You can attend at the court offices in person to make the request for judgment. Otherwise, you will need to send the court the following copies of Form N205A or N205B:

- The original request for the court files

- One copy for your own file

- One copy per defendant

The court will seal the original Form N205A or N205B and the copies of Form N205A or N205B. It will send one sealed copy to you, one to the defendant(s) and retain the original in the court file.

The debtor admits your <u>entire</u> claim, but without making any <u>offer</u> of payment

If this happens, you will need to apply to the court to enter judgment against the defendant. You need to tick box B of the tear-off part of Form N205A and tick the box at 'The defendant has not made any proposal for payment'. You should also tick the box in part C stating how you wish to be paid. Form N205B is much simpler but needs completing for claims for unspecified sums.

The debtor admits all of your claim and makes an offer to pay

If the defendant has accepted your claim, then he will have completed Form N9A or N9C. If the defendant makes an offer to pay that you are

Example Request for Judgment (Specified Amount) Form N205A

Notice of Issue
(specified amount)

In the

SWINDON COUNTY COURT

The court office at

To the Claimant ['s Solicitor]

(1) Brian Clarke

(2) Carol Clarke

Claim No.	SW065768
Claimant (include Ref.)	(1) Brian Clarke (2) Carol Clarke
Defendant(s)	Claybourne Building Services Ltd
Issue fee	£120

Your claim was issued on [18.04.06].
The court sent it to the defendant by first class post on [18.04.06]
and it will be deemed to be served on [20.04.06].
The defendant has until [04.05.06] to reply.

The defendant may
* Pay you your total claim.
* File an acknowledgment of service. This will allow the defendant 28 days from the date of service of your particulars of claim to file a defence or contest the court's jurisdiction.
* Dispute the whole claim. The court will send you a copy of the defence.
* Admit that all the money is owed. The defendant will send you a completed admission form and you may ask the court to enter judgment using the request below.

* Admit that only part of your claim is owed. The court will send you a copy of the reply form and you will have to decide what to do next.
* Not reply at all. You may ask the court to enter judgment using the request below.

Note: If the claim is disputed and the defendant is an individual, the claim may be transferred to the defendant's local court.

For further information please turn over

Request for Judgment

* Tick and complete either A or B. Remember to sign and date the form. Your signature certifies that the information you have given is correct.
* If the defendant has given an address on the form of admission to which correspondence should be sent, which is different from the address shown on the claim form, you must tell the court.
* Complete all the judgment details at C

In the

Claim No.	
Claimant (include Ref.)	
	(include Ref.)

A ☐ The defendant has not filed an admission or defence to my claim or an application to contest the court's jurisdiction.

Decide how and when you want the defendant to pay. You can ask for the judgment to be paid by instalments or in one payment.

B ☐ The defendant admits that all the money is owed
Tick only one box below and return the completed slip to the court.

☐ I accept the defendant's proposal for payment
Say how the defendant intends to pay. The court will send the defendant an order to pay. You will also be sent a copy.

☐ The defendant has not made any proposal for payment
Say how you want the defendant to pay. You can ask for the judgment to be paid by instalments or in one payment. The court will send the defendant an order to pay. You will also be sent a copy.

☐ I do NOT accept the defendant's proposal for payment
Say how you want the defendant to pay. Give your reasons for objecting to the defendant's offer of payment in Part D overleaf. Return this slip to the court with the defendant's admission (or a copy). The court will fix a rate of payment and send the defendant an order to pay. You will also be sent a copy.

I certify that the information given is correct

Signed .... Dated ....
(Claimant)(Claimant's Solicitor)(Litigation friend)

N205A Notice of issue (specified amount) and request for judgment

C Judgment details

I would like the defendant to be ordered to pay
☐ (immediately)
☐ (by instalments of £ .... per month)
☐ (in full by ....)

Amount of claim as stated in claim form
(including interest at date of issue) ....

Interest since date of claim (if any) ....
Period From .... To ....
Rate .... %

Court fees shown on claim ....
                                      Sub Total
Solicitor's costs (if any) on issuing claim ....
Solicitor's costs (if any) on entering judgment ....
                                      Sub Total
Deduct amount (if any) paid since issue
                                      Amount payable by defendant

prepared to accept, then you need to complete Form N205A and tick the first box in part B and the box 'I accept the defendant's proposal for payment'. The court will enter judgment and will let you and the defendant know by sending you Form N30.

It may be that you are happy with the defendant's admission but are unhappy about the proposal to pay by instalments. If so, you need to tick the box 'I do not accept the defendant's proposal for payment' and say why in part D on the reverse of the form. Remember to complete part C stating how you want the defendant to pay you. The defendant can offer to pay the money he admits to owing right away or offer to make monthly payments of the admitted sum and ask the court for time to pay. It is wise to look carefully at the defendant's Form N9A carefully since it sets out the details of the debtor's income and expenditure. Unless there is reason to doubt the truth of the contents, it will show you how realistic the defendant's offer is. If the debtor has little income and big commitments to other debts, children and/or other dependants, the court is likely to give him time to pay by instalments. It might be better to accept his offer than give the court an opportunity to order smaller payments over a longer period of time.

The debtor admits part of your claim

This means that the debtor considers he has a partial defence. The defendant should have completed Form N9 by ticking box 2 and then completed Form N9A. If you are happy to accept what the defendant offers, you should complete Form N225A and tick box B and the box at 'I accept the defendant's proposal for payment'. Remember that if you do so, you are accepting the defendant's offer to pay less, in full satisfaction of the whole claim.

If the defendant has admitted your claim and you have a judgment for the debt, you have only completed the easier part of your claim. If the defendant cannot, or is unwilling to, pay the judgment debt, the harder part is to enforce your debt. For further information, go to chapter 8.

Summary of entering judgment

Reason for application for judgment	Form required (Original form for court file and one copy for each claimant and defendant)	Judgment form sent by court
No Acknowledgment of Service Form was sent to the court by the defendant, where the claim is for **specified** sum of money	N205A – Request for Judgment	N30
No defence was sent to the court by the defendant, where the claim is for **specified** sum of money	N205A – Request for Judgment	N30
No Acknowledgment of Service Form was sent to the court by the defendant, where the claim is for **unspecified** sum of money	N205B – Request for Judgment	N30
No defence was sent to the court by the defendant, where the claim is for **unspecified** sum of money	N205B – Request for Judgment	N30
The defendant has admitted all the claim but made no offer to pay specified amount	N205A – Request for Judgment; or N225 – Request for Judgment and Reply to Admission	N30
The defendant has admitted all the claim and made an offer to pay that you accept	N205A – Request for Judgment; or N225 – Request for Judgment and Reply to Admission	N30(1)

Summary of entering judgment (continued)

The defendant has admitted all the claim and made an offer to pay that you do not accept	N205A – Request for Judgment; or N225 – Request for Judgment and Reply to Admission	N30(2)
The defendant has admitted part of the claim and made no offer to pay	N225A – Request for Judgment and Reply to Admission	Case proceeds as defended claim
The defendant has admitted part of the claim and made an offer to pay that you accept	N225A – Request for Judgment and Reply to Admission	N30(1)
The defendant has admitted part of the claim and made an offer to pay that you do not accept	N225A – Request for Judgment and Reply to Admission	Case proceeds as defended claim
The defendant has paid the sum claimed after you issued your Claim Form but did not pay your court costs	N225A – Request for Judgment and Reply to Admission	Case proceeds as defended claim
The defendant has failed to file an Acknowledgment of Service/Defence of your claim for unspecified amount of money (e.g. compensation for personal injury (pain and suffering) below £1,000)	N227 – Request for Judgment by Default	Court allocates case to Small Claims Track and directs assessment of damages or directs disposal hearing without allocation to a track

The debtor denies every bit of your claim

The debtor should have completed Form N9B, where you are claiming a specific sum of money, setting out what part of the claim he admits or denies and giving the details of his defence. If you are claiming unspecified compensation (e.g. for the pain and suffering caused by personal injury), the defendant should have completed Form N9D setting out the detail of his defence.

When the court receives a defence the court automatically transfers the case from the claimant's chosen court to the defendant's 'home' court. The defendant's home court is the one nearest to where he lives or works or carries on business. The court will notify both parties of the transfer. When the 'home' court receives the case file, it notifies both claimant and defendant. It is important to recall that the transfer is only automatic where the defendant is an individual as opposed to a limited company or partnership.

Evaluating the defence

The receipt of the defence is also the moment at which to ask yourself whether there is anything in it. You need to consider whether there are any significant points that you agree with or whether the defendant has attached any documents to his defence that prove his case. If he has, you may wish to negotiate a settlement of your dispute. If you consider there is nothing in the defence, then you may proceed.

An example is George Biddulph's defence, set out on Form N9B, on pages 83–4.

In Brian and Carol's case the case is not transferred. George is being sued as director of a limited company and they are already in the home court area of George Biddulph. When the court received George's defence it sent a copy to Brian and Carol.

Example Defence and Counterclaim Form N9B

Defence and Counterclaim (specified amount)

Name of court	Swindon County Court
Claim No.	SW065768
Claimant (including ref.)	Brian and Carol Clarke
Defendant	Claybourne Building Services Ltd Walnut Copse Peerpoint Housing Estate OXON OX5 6YY

- Fill in this form if you wish to dispute all or part of the claim and/or make a claim against the claimant (counterclaim).
- You have a limited number of days to complete and return this form to the court.
- Before completing this form, please read the notes for guidance attached to the claim form.
- Please ensure that all boxes at the top right of this form are completed. You can obtain the correct names and number from the claim form. The court cannot trace your case without this information.

How to fill in this form
- Complete sections 1 and 2. Tick the correct boxes and give the other details asked for.
- Set out your defence in section 3. If necessary continue on a separate piece of paper making sure that the claim number is clearly shown on it. In your defence you must state which allegations in the particulars of claim you deny and your reasons for doing so. **If you fail to deny an allegation it may be taken that you admit it.**
- If you dispute only some of the allegations you must
  - specify which you admit and which you deny; and
  - give your own version of events if different from the claimant's.

- If you wish to make a claim against the claimant (a counterclaim) complete section 4.
- Complete and sign section 5 before sending this form to the court. Keep a copy of the claim form and this form.

Community Legal Service Fund (CLSF)
You may qualify for assistance from the CLSF (this used to be called 'legal aid') to meet some or all of your legal costs. Ask about the CLSF at any county court office or any information or help point which displays this logo.

1. How much of the claim do you dispute?
- ☑ I dispute the full amount claimed as shown on the claim form

  or
- ☐ I admit the amount of £ _____

If you dispute only part of the claim you must **either**:
- pay the amount admitted to the person named at the address for payment on the claim form (see How to Pay in the notes on the back of, or attached to, the claim form). Then send this defence to the court

  or
- complete the admission form **and** this defence form and send them to the court.

  - ☐ I paid the amount admitted on (date) _____
  - **or**
  - ☐ I enclose the completed form of admission *(go to section 2)*

2. Do you dispute this claim because you have already paid it? *Tick whichever applies*
- ☑ No *(go to section 3)*
- ☐ Yes I paid £ _____ to the claimant
  on _____ *(before the claim form was issued)*

Give details of where and how you paid it in the box below *(then go to section 3)*

3. Defence

The work was carried out to a perfectly adequate standard for the type of installation that was supplied to the claimants at the price agreed.

The sum claimed for one broken handle is out of all proportion to the cost of its replacement. I deny the company is liable to pay the cost of another unnecessary builder.

Example Form N9B (continued)

Defence (continued)   Claim No. [   ]

4. If you wish to make a claim against the claimant (a counterclaim)

If your claim is for a specific sum of money, how much are you claiming? £ [   ]

I enclose the counterclaim fee of £ [   ]

My claim is for *(please specify nature of claim)*

- To start your counterclaim, you will have to pay a fee. Court staff can tell you how much you have to pay.

- You may not be able to make a counterclaim where the claimant is the Crown (e.g. a Government Department). Ask at your local county court office for further information.

What are your reasons for making the counterclaim?
If you need to continue on a separate sheet put the claim number in the top right hand corner

5. Signed
(To be signed by you or by your solicitor or litigation friend)

*(I believe)(The defendant believes) that the facts stated in this form are true. *I am duly authorised by the defendant to sign this statement

George Biddulph

*delete as appropriate

Position or office held (if signing on behalf of firm or company)

Managing Director

Defendant's date of birth, if an individual | 0 | 9 | M | 7 | 1 | 9 | 6 | 5

Date   24 April 2006

Give an address to which notices about this case can be sent to you

Walnut Copse
Peerpoint Housing Estate
OXON

Postcode OX5 6YY

Tel. no. **Mobile: 0770 090 0761**

if applicable

fax no.   01632 455 666

DX no.

e-mail   **mail@claybourne.com**

Completing the Allocation Questionnaire

Once it is clear that the defendant intends to contest the claim, the next stage is for the claimant and defendant to complete the Allocation Questionnaire. The court sends the Allocation Questionnaire after the defendant has filed a defence with the court and the claimant has informed the court that he wishes to proceed with the claim. Form N149 will arrive with a date marked in the top right-hand corner. This is the date by which the form must be completed and returned to the court. It is important to complete the form carefully because the court decides how much time to allot to the trial on the basis of the information given on the form. Page 4 of the form contains notes to assist you to complete it. Let us look at each section in turn.

A – Settlement

All courts try to encourage claimants and defendants to settle their disputes in order to comply with the overriding objective. Assuming you have already tried and failed to do so, you should tick the 'No' box. However, if there is a genuine negotiation occurring or you have arranged a mediation, it may be appropriate to consider ticking the 'Yes' box. Be aware, though, that once there is no hearing date looming, the pressure to settle is off the defendant. Your negotiation may benefit from the defendant knowing that the allocation is going ahead.

B – Location of hearing

The court in which the claim starts will not always be the one in which the trial takes place. This is because the court can order the transfer of a case to another court if it considers it would be more convenient or fair for the hearing to be in another court. The claim will probably be proceeding in the defendant's home court so the court will need a good reason to transfer the claim. You need to consider the following matters:

- Where you live
- Where the defendant is located

- How many witnesses you will be relying on at the trial
- Where the claimant and defendant witnesses are located

If the most convenient court is another court, it may be worth asking the court to transfer the case. It is worth checking with your witnesses and even telephoning the defendant to see if you can agree which court should hear the case. If there is more than one defendant, then the court will transfer to the home court of the first defendant provided he is an individual.

C – Track

All County Court claims are allocated to one of three 'tracks'. Look at the table below.

Allocation table

Track	Size of claim
Small claims track	Claims of £5,000 or below
	Personal injury claims for pain and suffering of £1,000 or less
	Landlord and tenant cases with compensation claims of £1,000 or less
Fast track	Claims with financial value of £15,000 or less
Multi-track	Other claims

At this stage it is worth recalling that the Small Claims Court is specifically used for hearing claims under £5,000. If your claim is in the small claims limit, you should tick the 'Yes' box. The District Judge has the power to order trial on another track if he considers it raises important legal or evidential issues that make it unsuitable for trial on the small claims track.

D – Witnesses

It is important to complete this correctly. The number of witnesses giving oral evidence will help the District Judge to decide how much time he should give your case when the trial date is fixed.

E – Experts

There will be more about expert witnesses later, but if you need an expert witness, you should ask the court for permission so tick the 'Yes' box. But the court will not give permission unless you clearly state **why** you need an expert witness in the Allocation Questionnaire. You must consider why the need for expert evidence arises. Usually it will be because the defendant does not accept what you say about some aspect of your case. For example, you may need expert evidence about the condition of a motor car when it was sold to you. If the defendant maintains that there was nothing wrong with the vehicle, then you will need expert evidence to prove the contrary. Similarly, if you are making a claim for personal injury and the defendant maintains that you have exaggerated the extent of your pain and suffering, you will need expert medical opinion.

If you already have your expert report, remember to attach a copy to the Allocation Questionnaire. Notice that the court wants to know if the defendant has seen the expert report. If the defendant has seen it but disagrees with what the expert says, then you can give this as a reason for the expert to attend court to give evidence.

F – Hearing

Make sure this part is completed as accurately as possible. District Judges will not be sympathetic to a hearing date being changed unless there is a good reason. This is because the court can only devote a certain amount of time to cases if it is to comply with the overriding objective. Changing dates for hearings involves the court staff in using administrative time that could have been spent elsewhere. If you need an interpreter, you need to inform the court. This is because the court may need to allocate a larger office for the hearing so that there are the correct number of seats. The notes at page 4 suggest that the court can pay the costs of an interpreter and they give the web address for checking this out. Unless you fall into this category, however, you must pay for the interpreter.

G – Other information

This space gives you the opportunity to assist the court by flagging up anything that affects the progress of the claim that has not already been thought about; for example, if the defendant could but has failed to give you information that might help you decide to stop the claim, you can say so here. You may feel that the defence document does not really give sufficient detail to explain the defence or you may feel that the District Judge hearing the case should make a site visit. If this is the case, you should say so in the box provided on the form.

Disability issues

Section G of the form is a good place to raise disability issues. The Customer Services Officer (CSO) of the court can help with access to the court building, but it is wise to notify the CSO in advance of the trial if disability issues need to be addressed. It might be that one of your witnesses is 'non-ambulant' and needs wheelchair access and appropriate space at the District Judge's table. If you have arranged language interpreters, you need to warn the court so that an appropriate size of room and correct number of seats can be arranged for the hearing.

H – Fee

You must attach payment for filing the Allocation Questionnaire before you return the form to the court. If you do not, the court will not allocate the case to a track and issue directions for progressing your claim. There is no allocation fee for claims under £1,500. Alternatively, you can get up-to-date information about this at www.hmcourts-service.gov.uk.

Example Allocation Questionnaire Form N149

Allocation questionnaire
(Small claims track)

In the
SWINDON
County Court

Completed by, or on behalf of, (print name)

Brian and Carol Clarke

Claim No.	SW065768
Last date for filing with court office	17 May 2006

who is the [Claimant][Defendant] in this claim.

Please read the notes on page 4 before completing the questionnaire.

You must complete this questionnaire. It will be used to assist the court in the management of the claim.

You should note the date by which it must be returned and the name of the court it should be returned to since this may be different from the court where proceedings were issued. This information is shown on the Form N152 which came with this questionnaire.

If you have settled this claim (or if you settle it on a future date) and therefore do not need a hearing, you must let the court know immediately.

A Settlement

Do you wish any further action in this claim to be postponed for one month so that you and the other party can attempt to settle the claim either by informal discussion or by alternative dispute resolution?   ☐ Yes ☑ No

B Location of hearing

The claim will be heard in the court to which this form must be returned. Is there any reason why it should be transferred to another court to be heard?   ☐ Yes ☑ No

If Yes, say which court and why

C Track

Do you agree that the small claims track is the most suitable track for this claim?   ☑ Yes ☐ No

If No, please say why

N149 Allocation questionnaire (Small claims tracks) (11.05) 1   HMCS

Example Allocation Questionnaire Form N149 (continued)

D Witnesses

So far as you know at this stage, how many witnesses (other than yourself) do you intend to call to give evidence at the hearing?

> 2

E Experts

Do you want permission to use an expert's report at the hearing? *(see notes)* ☐ Yes ☑ No

If Yes, what will the expert's evidence deal with?

Have you already obtained an expert's report? ☐ Yes ☑ No

If Yes, have you given a copy of that report to the other party? ☐ Yes ☐ No

In addition to using an expert's report do you want your expert to attend the hearing and give evidence? ☐ Yes ☐ No

If Yes, give the reasons why you think their attendance is necessary:

The court may order the appointment of a single expert who can be instructed by both parties. If you think this would not be appropriate, please say why.

F Hearing

Are there any days within the next four months when you, an expert or a witness will not be able to attend court for the hearing? ☐ Yes ☑ No

If Yes, please give details

	Dates not available
Yourself	
Expert	
Other essential witness	

Will you be using an interpreter at the hearing either for yourself or for a witness? *(see notes)* ☐ Yes ☑ No

If Yes, please specify the type of interpreter

Example Allocation Questionnaire Form N149 (continued)

G Other information

In the space below, set out any other information you consider will help the judge to manage or clarify the claim, including any other information you consider should be supplied by the other party.

> We attach a set of the photographs we have taken of the conservatory the defendant installed. We have sent them to the defendant.

H Fee

Have you attached the fee for filing this allocation questionnaire? ☐ Yes ☑ No

I Signature *(see notes)*

Signed *Brian Clarke*   *Carol Clarke*   Date 28 April 2006

Print full name Brian and Carol Clarke

If a solicitor is acting for you please enter the firm's name, reference number and full postal address including (if appropriate) details of fax number, e-mail address, Document Exchange (DX) number. Otherwise, please enter your details as appropriate. This will assist the court in contacting you, if necessary at short notice.

	Ref. no.	
	Telephone no.	
	Mobile no.	
	Fax no.	
	e-mail address	
	DX no.	

3

I – Signature

If you sign the form, your claim can progress to the next stage. Conversely, if you do not, your claim will not progress. Be sure, therefore, to take this step.

An example of Form N149 that Brian and Carol completed is shown on pages 89–91.

When the court has received the Allocation Questionnaire from both parties it will:

- allocate the case to a track;

- send a copy of the completed defendant Allocation Questionnaire to the claimant and a copy of the completed claimant questionnaire to each defendant;

- send a copy of Form N157 to each claimant and defendant.

Brian and Carol received Form N157 from the Swindon County Court informing them that their case had been listed for hearing on the small claims track on 4 June 2006. An example of Form N157 can be found on the following page.

There are a few things to notice about this form:

- **The hearing date**

  The court has fixed the date for the trial. If this is not a suitable date, you must write to the court **immediately**.

- **The estimated length of hearing**

  The court allocates the amount of time it considers to be appropriate to hear the case in accordance with the overriding objective. If you have reason to doubt that the time is sufficient, you must inform the court at once and say why you disagree with the time estimate. In practice, however, the court is experienced in setting aside the right amount of time for each individual case. But the more information you give the court at allocation stage about your claim the more accurate the time estimate will be.

- **The directions**

  After the time estimate the form has a list of 'directions'. Directions are

Example Defence Form N157

Notice of Allocation to the Small Claims Track	In the **SWINDON COUNTY COURT**

Claim No.	SW065768
Claimant (including ref)	(1) Brian Clarke (2) Carol Clarke
Defendant (including ref)	Claybourne Building Services Ltd
Date	09/05/2006

To [Claimant] [Defendant] [& Solicitor]

(1) Brian Clarke

(2) Carol Clarke

Seal

District Judge   Wellfield   has considered the statements of case and allocation questionnaires
filed and allocated the claim [counterclaim] to the Small Claims Track.

The hearing, of this claim [counterclaim] will take place at 2   [am][pm]on the 4th of June 2006
at The Law Courts, Islington Street, Swindon

The judge has estimated that the hearing, of this claim [counterclaim] should take no longer than

[1.5 xmins][hours]. This is the total time for you, the other party [parties] and any, witnesses to put your
evidence for the judge to reach a decision. To help prepare the claim [counterclaim] for hearing, the judge
has ordered that you comply, with the following directions:-

1. Each party shall deliver to every other party and to the court office copies of all documents (including any expert's report) on which he intends to rely at the hearing no later than [22 May 2006] [14 days prior to the hearing].
2. The original documents shall be brought to the hearing.
3. The court must be informed immediately if the case is settled by agreement before the hearing date.
4. Signed statements setting out the evidence of all witnesses on whom each party relies shall be prepared and included in the documents mentioned in paragraph 1. This includes the evidence of the parties themselves and any other witnesses.

[The reason[s] the judge has given for allocation to this track [is][are] that   .]

The value of the claim is below £5,000
Suitable for Small Claims Track

Notes

- If you cannot, or choose not to, attend the hearing, you must write and tell the court at **least 7 days before the date of the hearing.** The district judge will hear the case in your absence, but will take account of your statement of case and any, other documents you have filed.

- If you do not attend the hearing, and do not give notice that You will not attend, the district judge may strike out your claim, defence or counter claim. If the claimant attends but the defendant does not, the district judge may make a decision based on the evidence of the claimant only.

- Leaflets explaining more about what You should do and what happens when your case is allocated to the small claims track are available from the court office.

The court office at The Law Courts, Islington Street, SWINDON

is open between 10 am and 4 pm Monday to Friday. Address all communications to the Court Manager quoting the claim number
N157 Notice of Allocation to the Small Claims Track

steps the claimant and the defendant must take to prepare the case for trial. They are very practical steps designed to make sure both claimant and defendant know the details of each other's position. The reason for this is that English law requires parties to put their 'cards face up on the table' in the interests of fairness and to assist the court to arrive at a just decision. It is important to remember that the courts derive their authority from the Crown, i.e. the reigning monarch. This is why you will see the Royal Coat of Arms on the wall of the court building. All judges swear an oath to dispense the Crown's justice in accordance with the law and procedure and in a way that is just. Every step you are required to take helps the District Judge to do so.

The directions will vary according to what type of small claim you are making. The County Court uses the following sets of standard directions:

- Form A – The standard directions

- Form B – Standard directions for use in claims arising out of road traffic accidents

- Form C – Standard directions for use in claims arising out of building disputes, vehicle repairs and similar contractual claims

- Form D – Tenants' claims for the return of deposits/landlords' claims for damage caused

- Form E – Holiday and wedding claims

All the standard directions have the following common features:

- The evidence upon which a claimant or a defendant relies must be served on the other side within a fixed period of time of the trial date. This means supplying copies of any documents you will be using at the trial.

- The original documents must be brought to court on the day of the trial.

- The court must be informed if the dispute is settled before the trial date.

Complying with the directions is the first step to preparing the case for trial, the subject of the next chapter.

CHAPTER 5
The trial

Preparing for trial

There is a trite saying which goes, 'Fail to prepare, prepare to fail'. It really brings home the importance of preparing for events. It is no less true of a small claim. But preparation for a hearing in the Small Claims Court is only a series of small steps. In this chapter we shall look at each of those steps.

The first step is to ascertain what the directions are. Most cases are relatively straightforward and so the court issues, what it calls, 'standard directions' after the allocation stage. The standard directions are as follows:

1. Each party shall deliver to every other party and to the court office copies of all documents (including any expert's report) on which he intends to rely at the hearing no later than [......] [*14 days before the hearing*].

2. The original documents shall be brought to the hearing.

3. [*Notice of hearing date and time allowed.*]

4. The court must be informed immediately if the case is settled by agreement before the hearing date.

What do directions 1 and 2 mean?

Direction 1

If you are relying on a document, such as a contract, to prove that you entered a legally binding agreement, then you must send a copy of it to each defendant or claimant. You must also send copies to the court. The same is true of any other document you rely upon, including an expert report. It is essential to send them within the time limit set out by the court. If you fail to do so, the District Judge may refuse to allow you to rely upon those documents at the trial, because the defendant will not have seen them beforehand.

Direction 2

Although you may send copies of your documents to the other side and the court you must prove that the copies are genuine by turning up with the original document at court. If there is a good reason why the original is not available, you can explain this to the District Judge. The District Judge has the power to accept your document as credible evidence of the existence of the original item. This is because the strict rules of evidence do not apply to a small claim. However, it does not mean that you do not have to prove what you say. If you are claiming that you made a contract with the defendant, you will have to prove it by producing the original contract or some proof the agreement was made.

Additional directions

The court can make additional directions, if they are appropriate and proportionate.

Brian and Carol received Form A Standard Directions from the Swindon County Court, but one more direction was added to the standard list: '5. Signed statements setting out the evidence of all witnesses on whom each party intends to rely shall be prepared and included in the documents mentioned in paragraph 1. This includes the evidence of the parties themselves and any other witnesses.'

Compliance with court directions

Expert witnesses

Some claims require the assistance of an expert witness. An expert witness is someone who has special knowledge, skills and experience of a particular field of expertise. An expert witness is also someone who is prepared to share his expertise with the court in order to explain some of the evidence. He is not necessarily a person who is academically qualified in a narrow field. An expert can be a competent plumber who has been a plumber for a long time. Such a plumber is likely to be able to deal with most problems that come his way and explain why a particular problem can occur. He is likely to be able to express an opinion on the quality of work carried out by others simply because he is very able and has been around long enough to know a good from a bad job. Experts who give evidence in Small Claims Courts can be:

- Architects
- Builders
- Designers
- Doctors and dentists
- Electricians
- Engineers
- Furniture makers
- Joiners and cabinet makers
- Plumbers
- Surveyors
- Upholsterers

If the court gave you permission to call expert evidence, the directions will inform you about serving that evidence on the defendant. Do ensure that you have complied with the court direction.

Witness statements

The witness statement is used to tell the court your side of the story and to explain why you want the money you have claimed. It is a good idea to make one even if you have not been asked by the court to do so because it will help you to have a coherent record of the events that led to your claim. It will help to refresh your memory of what happened when you give your evidence in court.

Remember the six serving men:

'My master kept six serving men; they taught me all I knew,
Their names were what and why and when and how and where and who.'

These two lines of poetry remind us that finding out about anything starts with these simple questions. When you write a witness statement try to remember them.

The timeline

Begin by making a timeline to give you a sequence of events. This will help you to get all the relevant events into the right date order. If the events concern the months between May 2004 and September 2005, try creating a table and inputting the events. Look at the example below:

Month	Event
May 2004	Contract for supply of 1,000 PCBs. Order number 04/6379.
June 2004	PCBs delivered to customer (delivery note 04/1745). Terms and conditions on back of delivery note.
July 2004	Invoice 04/9871 – terms and conditions on back.
August 2004	Fresh order number 04/7289 for PCBs.
September 2004	Delivered to customer. Delivery note 04/4587 – terms and conditions on reverse.
October 2004	Invoice 04/10006 – terms on reverse.
November 2004	Fresh order number 04/8652 – terms on reverse.

December 2004	Delivered to customer (delivery note 04/5794 – terms on reverse).
January 2005	Invoice 05/0000231 – terms on reverse.
February 2005	Order 04/8652 sent back by customer; rejected for defects. Standard letter sent demanding payment. Defects to be drawn to our attention within seven days of delivery.
March 2005	Customer says our terms do not apply – see letter 04/03/05.
April 2005	Our call to customer to chase debt. See scratchpad note on database 05/04/8652. DH telling JT that our terms apply because we have supplied three times on them. Credit note for so called faulty components refused.

Insert the events for each month in the right-hand column and make a note of the document that proves the event. You can then write the witness statement knowing you will get everything in the correct sequential order. You can then insert more of the detail so that the court knows what was said or done by whom, when and where. It is more tedious than difficult.

Remember that good witness statements:

- are written in plain English using short sentences, and correct punctuation and spelling. However, no court will penalise anyone who does not do so. The court's job is to examine the facts and apply the law. It is not an essay competition;

- are written in legible script. If you are using a word processor, some fonts are easier to read than others. Use the font that is easy to read. Use the paragraph setting for 1.5 lines as this makes type easier to read. If you are writing by hand, make sure it is clear and easy to read;

- are no longer than necessary to inform the court about the facts. They are not repetitive. When you have explained one matter move on to the next;

- progress in a logical sequence from one event to another;

- show the court why you are entitled to the money you are claiming;

- stick to the facts (the six serving men);
- dwell only on relevant matters, with no opinion, emotion or feelings.

The statement of truth

All witness statements must conclude with a statement of truth to verify the contents. The court rules state that at the end of the statement you must say:

'I believe the facts stated in this witness statement are true.'

Look at the statements of Brian and Carol.

I, Mr Brian Clarke, STATE as follows:

1. I am Brian Clarke and I live with my wife and two children at Sheiling Lawn Cottage, Bays Lane, OXON OX9 3PP. In September 2005 my wife and I decided we needed more space.

2. We asked George Biddulph of Claybourne Building Services Ltd to quote for installing a standard type of modular UPVC conservatory with thermal performance glass. I attach his estimate for carrying out the work dated 11 October 2005.

3. The work began on 5 November 2005. Before it began I gave Mr Biddulph half of the total price. I attach a copy of my bank statement showing the transfer of £7,500 from my account on 8 November.

4. The work on building the conservatory was completed in three weeks and I paid Mr Biddulph the balance of £7,500 on 28 November 2005. I attach a copy of our joint building society account book showing the withdrawal by cheque of £7,500. We were pleased with the conservatory because we had been so short of space, but by the beginning of December, the following week, it was raining hard and we noticed the following:

    - Leaks in the roof panels. (We had to put a bucket under it and the bucket remained there between December 2005 and February 2006.)

- Leaky double door letting in rain from the garden. (We had to keep towels there to soak up the water.)

- Plaster under a window cracking and 'blown' from water seeping in from outside.

- Handle on fanlight window would not lock.

5. I attach an envelope to this statement. The envelope contains photographs that I took with my Minolta Micro 452 digital camera on Sunday 29 January 2006. The photographs show the defects.

6. I telephoned Mr Biddulph on Friday 2 December 2005 and told him what had happened. He seemed sympathetic and he said that he would send one of his lads round the next morning. No one came and I could not get hold of Mr Biddulph again until I spoke with him on the telephone at around 4.00pm on Wednesday 7 December. I remember it was that day because I was doing a late shift at work and I had to phone him in my break. Mr Biddulph again expressed sympathy but did not come round the following Saturday morning as promised.

7. I tried to contact Mr Biddulph again at the following times:

- Monday 12 December 2005 at 8.30am but his mobile phone was switched off.

- Monday 12 December 2005 at 12 noon at his office. His phone was not answered.

- Monday 12 December 2005 at 6.00pm at his home address. His wife answered the phone and said that he was not there.

- Tuesday 13 December 2005 at 7.30am. His wife answered the phone and said that he had already gone to the office.

- Tuesday 13 December 2005 at 7.45am at the office. The answerphone was on. I left a message for him to contact me.

- Wednesday 14 December 2005 at 12 noon at his office. Carol spoke with him and he told her he would come and see us at 6.00pm that evening.

8. Mr Biddulph did not turn up and so I telephoned him at home at 6.30pm but as usual his wife said he was not in. Then I was

> very busy over the Christmas period until I telephoned him on 9 January 2006. Mr Biddulph told me that there was nothing wrong with the work he had carried out and I should just replace the broken handle with one from the DIY store. I informed him that unless he put right what was wrong by the end of the week I would get another builder to put it right and send him the bill. Mr Biddulph said I could do what I liked!
>
> 9. I attach a copy of the bill we received from Gary Kimble of 4Walls Maintenance Company Ltd to put right the various defects. I ask the court to order the defendant to pay it and to give us the interest we have lost and our costs.
>
> 10. I believe the facts stated in this witness statement are true.
>
> *Brian Clarke*

Here is the statement of Carol Clarke. Notice that she simply confirms what her husband has related in his witness statement, at the times at which she was present.

> I, Carol Clarke, STATE as follows:
>
> 1. I am the wife of Brian Clarke and I live with him and our two children at our home at Sheiling Lawn Cottage, Bays Lane, OXON OX9 3PP.
>
> 2. I have read the statement of my husband Brian Clarke and can confirm everything he says in paragraphs 1 to 4, 7, 8 and 9.
>
> 3. I believe the facts stated in this witness statement are true.
>
> *Carol Clarke*

Here is the statement of their witness, Mr Gary Kimble. Mr Kimble has the tricky task of showing how his evidence is reliable and is not just given out of self-interest. But notice how he sticks to the facts and proves each statement by referring to his observations and the photographic evidence.

I, Gary Kimble, STATE as follows:

1. I am the proprietor of 4Walls Maintenance Company Ltd of 2 Tracey Drive, Horn Lane, OXON OX5 7AP. I have been a builder for the last 35 years and all my customers are from the area in which I live. I do only domestic building and maintenance work.

2. On 20 January 2006 I was asked by the claimant, Brian Clarke, to call at his home to examine some defects in the conservatory at his home. I went to take a look at it on Saturday 21 January as I do all my estimating on Saturday mornings.

3. Mr and Mrs Clarke told me that the conservatory leaked and that some of the plaster and brickwork had salts coming through the surface. They complained of water ingress through the roof and French windows. They informed me that the conservatory had been fitted in November 2005.

4. I examined the whole of the installation. I always do this because what householders think is the root of a problem may be caused by something else. The weather was dry when I examined the conservatory but I noticed the following:

    (a) **The glass roof panels:** Two glass roof panels were not securely bedded between the UPVC roof struts (photographs 2 and 3). There was clear evidence of water penetration because there was mildew and mould between the glass and the struts where the mastic seal was incomplete. The floor beneath the panels showed the presence of water stains. The incomplete seal on the roof panels made me cautious about the other seals and so I examined the mastic seals on the rest of the roof panels, which I found to be in order. I recommended that the two roof panels should be removed and the mould and mildew be treated so that the panels could be rebedded and properly sealed.

    (b) **The left exterior window:** I then looked at the exterior seals to the windows. Photographs 5 and 6 show the exterior window to the left of the French doors leading onto the patio. I looked at the underside surface of the interior cill. I noticed it was damp and that moisture had penetrated from the exterior wall. I examined the exterior seal of the window and found that the seal was again incomplete. I concluded that it was the cause of the water penetration and recommended remedial action, which simply meant removing the old seal and applying a new one.

(c) **The French windows:** The claimants complained of water ingress through the bottom of the French windows (photographs 7 and 8). When I examined them I noticed there was a visible gap of about 0.75cm, sufficiently large to permit water penetration. The gap can clearly be seen on photograph 8. The water stains of the floor tiles suggested there had been water ingress. I examined the rest of the door frame to ascertain why the gap was present and observed the doors were not level owing to the position of the door hinges. I recommended that the doors be removed and rehung to alter the position of the doors appropriately.

(d) **The left interior window plaster work (photographs 9 and 10):** The plaster was cracked and showed significant water penetration since it was 'blown'. This means that the surface was blistered and cracking. The salts from the plaster had accumulated onto the surface area causing the paint finish to flake and crack too. I concluded that water penetration caused by the incomplete seal had caused the damage. I recommended removing the damaged plaster and reinstating it with new plaster with damp resister incorporated into it.

(e) **The fanlight window handle (photograph 11):** This was broken and while it could be used for opening and shutting the window it would not lock so that the window could not be left secure. The handle is part of a complete set that comes with this particular modular conservatory. It is called the 'Carmen Suite' set but is no longer manufactured in Portugal by the supplier. I recommended that it be replaced with a new handle but I could not find one similar to the rest of the set. Mr and Mrs Clarke instructed me to replace all the handles for all the conservatory fittings.

Carol's letter to defendant listing the documents

**Brian and Carol Clarke, Sheiling Lawn Cottage,
Bays Lane, Oxon OX9 3PP**

George Biddulph
Claybourne Building Services Ltd
Walnut Copse
Peerpoint Housing Estate
Oxon OX5 6YY

6 May 2006

Dear Mr Biddulph,

Our Conservatory – Court Hearing – Claim Number SW065768

The court has ordered us to send you copies of our documents before the trial. We enclose the following documents in support of our case:

1. Copy of your estimate dated 11 October 2005.
2. Copy of your invoice dated 14 November 2005.
3. Copy of our letter of 6 April 2006.
4. Copy of 4Walls Maintenance Company invoice dated 2 February 2006.
5. Photographs of the conservatory before it was repaired.
6. Notes of our telephone calls with you.
7. Copy of witness statement of Gary Kimble of 4Walls Maintenance Company Ltd.
8. Copy of witness statement of Brian Clarke.
9. Copy of witness statement of Carol Clarke.

Please confirm that you have received our documents. We are happy for you to confirm receipt by email. Please also tell us if you agree with Gary Kimble's statement so we know if he will have to come to court.

Yours sincerely,

Brian and Carol Clarke

cc Swindon County Court

> (f) **The remedial works** to the conservatory were carried out by me on 2 February 2006.
>
> **5.** I believe the facts stated in this witness statement are true.
>
> *Gary Kimble*

Documents

You need to send copies of all the documents you will use to support your case to the court. Make a list and put that list on a covering letter to the court. When you send your copy documents to the defendant it is a good idea to send them with a covering letter listing the items you have sent. Ask the defendant to let you know that he has received them. You need to be able to prove that you have complied with the court directions if necessary. A good way is to copy the letter to the defendant to the court. Remember too that you must comply with the directions within the time limits set down by the court.

In our example, Carol made a list of their documents to send to George Biddulph and wrote a letter to him enclosing the documents (see previous page). But Brian and Carol must also show that they have complied with the court directions **inside the time limits**. The letter Carol wrote to the court can be found on the following page.

The court will date stamp the letter and the documents when it receives them so there will be a court record of compliance with the directions.

Agreeing witness evidence

Whilst claimants are able to propel themselves to court at the appointed time, other witnesses may not be so keen. Furthermore, it involves time and expense. If you need an expert witness, you will have to pay an expert to prepare the report and to give evidence at the trial. The directions oblige you to send a copy of any document you rely upon to the defendant so you should see if the defendant agrees with your evidence. This can be done by asking the defendant, by letter or over the phone.

Carol's letter to the court listing the documents

Brian and Carol Clarke, Sheiling Lawn Cottage, Bays Lane, Oxon OX9 3PP

Swindon County Court
The Law Courts
Islington Street
Swindon SN1 2HG

6 May 2006

Dear Sir,

Brian and Carol Clarke v Claybourne Building Services Ltd – Claim Number SW065768 – Trial Date 4 June 2006

We were ordered to send the court copies of the documents we will be using to support our claim. We enclose the following:

1. A copy of an estimate from Claybourne Building Services Ltd dated 11 October 2005.

2. A copy of an invoice from Claybourne Building Services Ltd dated 14 November 2005.

3. A copy of a letter from the claimant to the defendant dated 6 April 2006.

4. A copy of an invoice from 4Walls Maintenance Company Ltd dated 2 February 2006.

5. Photographs of the conservatory before it was repaired.

6. Notes of our telephone calls between the claimant and defendant.

7. A copy of a witness statement by Gary Kimble of 4Walls Maintenance Company Ltd.

8. A copy of Brian Clarke's witness statement.

9. A copy of Carol Clarke's witness statement.

We have sent copies by post to the defendant today.

Yours faithfully,

Brian and Carol Clarke

Enc.

cc George Biddulph

Getting witnesses to court

You need to ensure that all your witnesses know when the trial date is. Only the claimant and the defendant will be notified by the court of the trial date after the case's allocation to the Small Claims Court, so you need to ensure that your witnesses are aware of the date and that they are available. Warn your witnesses of the time of the trial and also how long before the trial you would like them to be at court. Make sure that your witnesses also have a copy of their own witness statement and any other documents they need to refresh their memory. Remind the witnesses of any original documents they may need to bring to court. Help your witnesses to get to court by downloading the location maps available from the Court Service website.

This is also a good time to find out if your witness has ever given evidence to a court before. If not, help your witness by sending him information about being a witness. You can download leaflets EX341 and EX342 from the Court Service website. It will give you guidance on what is expected of a witness and what will happen when he comes to court. Details of claiming witness expenses are also given.

Assembling your evidence

It is important that you feel confident that you have everything you need at your fingertips in court. Even a small claim can create a good volume of paper. It can be helpful to put together an A4 ring-binder file with the following in it:

- N1 Claim Form
- Claim supporting documents
- N9 Defence Form or N11
- Defendant supporting documents
- Claimant's witness statement
- Other supporting witness statements
- Defendant's witness statement

- Other supporting witness statements

You can 'flag' the documents and label the flags to help you find them quickly.

If you are using photographs, it is best to mount them into a small album and number them so everyone in court will know which photographs are being discussed.

Some types of claim lend themselves to other sorts of visual aids for helping the court to understand the facts. Here are some items that can be helpful to a Small Claims Court:

Type of case	Visual aids
Personal injury	<ul><li>Video footage or photographs of the scene of the accident.</li><li>Models of body parts to show where the injury occurred.</li><li>Drawings or photographs of affected body parts to show injury.</li></ul>
Road accident/ property damage	<ul><li>Sketch drawings of location of accident.</li><li>Photographs of location.</li><li>Toy cars for demonstrating collisions.</li><li>Photographs of physical damage to vehicle/property.</li></ul>
Contract/ Recovery of fees	<ul><li>Sample of subject of contract if it is unusual or would be helpful (e.g. a wall tie, drawings of location of contract).</li><li>Diagram of house or other installation to show the different parts and photographs of work carried out, if the claim happens to be about work which was carried out on a property.</li></ul>

Knowing your case

It is important that you know your documents and those of the defendant forwards, backwards and inside out. The better you know them, the better you know your case and the easier you will find it to explain it to the District Judge. If you tell the District Judge about a contract you made, you need to tell him where he will find the contract. You could say, 'Sir, a copy of the contract is attached to the Claim Form.'

Practising your case

There is little in life that does not improve with practice and the same is true of your small claim. While the small claims procedure aims to be simple, informal and as unlike a trial as it can be, it is still a formal procedure. It is natural for people who are unused to it to feel intimidated. Thankfully, District Judges understand this very well and will do their utmost to put court users at ease. Yet it will still help you if you can get a close friend or relative to listen to you explain your case, as though you were in front of the District Judge. Ask your friend to be honest about whether you got your point across clearly.

You do not have to learn a speech. It is better to simply tell the District Judge why you are there. Good 'ice-breakers' to get you started are lines such as:

'I am here today because…'

'I want the court to order the defendant to [……] because [……]…'

'I am the claimant and…'

'This trial is about an accident I had on [date] when…'

You do not have to use legal language. It is better if you tell the District Judge simply and plainly why you are in court and why you think he should give you judgment against the defendant.

Explanations should follow a logical progression from one thing to another; for example, in a contract case:

'I made a contract with the defendant. You can see a copy of it attached to my Claim Form. Under the contract I agreed [...] and he agreed [...]. But when the time came for [....] the defendant [*did/did not do* ...]. I am claiming [...] because [......]. I have read what the defendant says in his defence. It is not true because [......].'

Using your witness statement

If you have prepared a complete witness statement, you can ask the District Judge if he will regard your witness statement as your oral evidence. Then add that you are happy to answer any questions about it from the District Judge or from the defendant.

The day of the trial

On the day of the trial there a number of steps you can take to ensure that things go smoothly. If you are not taking public transport, you need to ascertain where you will park. Do not assume that there will be a car park at the court or that court users will be allowed into it. Many courts have no car parks or have restricted access to them.

Dressing appropriately

You are not expected to turn up dressed like a lawyer. It is not necessary to wear a suit, especially if you are not used to wearing a suit and tie. It is far better to attend court wearing clean, tidy clothes that are not too flamboyant. The District Judge will be used to seeing all kinds of attire. He is more interested in what you have to say than how you are dressed. However, he is human too and he will gain some impressions from how you appear. Clean, ironed clothes and polished shoes are likely to create a good impression that suggests you treat the court seriously.

Arriving early

It is sensible to arrive early. Allow yourself at least 30 minutes prior to the trial time. You will need this simply to acquaint yourself with the building, find the court usher and the toilets. (Do not underestimate the effect of nerves!) You may also need to meet your witness.

Finding the court usher

Ushers are easily identified because they wear a black gown. They are there to help the court users by directing them to the correct court, or to other parts of the building. They are generally very experienced at assisting the public and are a mine of useful information. The ushers have copies of the court list so they know where to direct you.

Remember to keep an ear trained on the tannoy if cases are being called via a tannoy.

Conduct of the small claims hearing

The court rules state that the Small Claims Court:

- may adopt any method of proceeding at a hearing that it considers fair;
- will conduct hearings informally;
- need not apply the strict rules of evidence;
- need not ask witnesses to give evidence on oath;
- may limit cross-examination;
- must give reasons for its decision.

The flexibility of the court rules mean that different District Judges adopt different ways of conducting a hearing. Some District Judges are very 'hands-on' and try to get the claimant and defendant to agree a settlement between them. Others will adopt a more formal approach. This is because further court rules state that the judge may:

- ask questions of any witnesses himself before allowing anyone else to do so;

- only permit cross-examination when all the witnesses have given 'evidence-in-chief';

- limit 'cross-examination' to a particular subject or issue over a fixed period of time.

Here are some methods used by District Judges to hear small claims:

Method	Procedure
1 – Normal sequence	• Claimant gives his evidence. • Defendant cross-examines the claimant. • Claimant calls witness(es). • Defendant cross-examines claimant's witness(es). • Claimant closes case. • Defendant gives his evidence. • Claimant cross-examines defendant. • Defendant calls witness(es). • Claimant cross-examines defendant's witness(es). • Defendant closes case. • District Judge asks any questions. • District Judge makes reasoned decision.
2 – Shorter sequence	• The District Judge tells both claimant and defendant that he has read all the papers and witness statements before the hearing. The District Judge summarises the positions of the claimant and defendant. The District Judge asks the claimant and defendant if his summary is correct. • Claimant and the claimant's witness(es) all give evidence.

	• Defendant and the defendant's witness(es) all give evidence.
	• Claimant cross-questions the defendant's witness(es).
	• Defendant cross-questions the claimant's witness(es).
	• Claimant and defendant are given five minutes each to say why the court should make the decision in their favour.
	• District Judge makes a reasoned decision.
3 – 'Hands-on' sequence	• District Judge explains what he has read and explains the relevant law including what legal matters he has discounted right away as irrelevant to his decision.
	• District Judge gives the claimant and defendant a fixed amount of time to tell their own story and say why the claim should be decided in their favour.
	• District Judge asks questions of the witness(es).
	• Witness(es) give evidence.
	• District Judge allows claimant and defendant to cross-question each other's witness(es).
	• District Judge makes a reasoned decision.

There are other variations too. Whatever method the District Judge adopts, remember that you will always have an opportunity to tell your story and ask the defendant and his witnesses any questions you have.

About the courtroom

Generally small claims are heard in a District Judge's office. Occasionally, only a formal court is available. If this happens, the District Judge will probably not sit on the raised bench but at the desk in front of the bench. Then he will ask the claimant and defendant to sit in front of the desk he is at.

The running order

When you go into the District Judge's room the District Judge will greet you and ask you who you are and direct you to seats at the table in front of him. The District Judge will ask the claimant, defendant and anyone else present to identify themselves. Then he will explain how the case will run. The practice can vary from one District Judge to another. In general, however, he will tell you:

- the purpose of the hearing;
- the powers of the court;
- what order the proceedings will take, i.e. who will speak first, second, etc., and that interruptions are not permitted;
- what he understands the issues between the parties to be;
- the relevant law if the legal issues are clear;
- that the claimant must prove his case on the balance of probability;
- that he must give reasons for his decision;
- what you can do if you do not like the decision.

Addressing the District Judge/Judge

It is usually a District Judge who hears a small claim. Sometimes the Resident Circuit Judge will hear a small claim if he has finished his own work and has some spare time. Look at the table below as to how to address them.

Title	How they are addressed
Circuit Court Judge (male or female)	Your Honour
District Judge (male)	Sir
District Judge (female)	Madam or Ma'm

Telling the court your story (examination-in-chief)

You can do this either by reading out your witness statement, if you have made one, or by simply telling the court about the events that brought you to court. The same is just as true of a defendant who is giving 'evidence-in-chief'. You may find the District Judge interrupting you from time to time with questions. However, the District Judge will not permit the defendant to interrupt the claimant or the claimant to interrupt the defendant. Sometimes the District Judge will only ask questions after the 'evidence-in chief' is complete.

Here is how Brian gave his evidence-in-chief:

'My name is Brian Clarke. I live with my wife and our two children at our home in Sheiling Lawn Cottage, Bays Lane. We like living there, but until we had the conservatory built it was quite cramped. We decided to add a conservatory to the sitting room. The sitting room faces out onto the garden and we thought it would be a good place to put all the children's toys for them to play in. We told George Biddulph what we wanted and why. He told us the conservatory would be just fine for what we had in mind. He gave us a quote for doing the work dated 11 October 2005. We went to him because he was doing a job a few doors away. He came to quote while his lads were working on the neighbour's house. You can see the quote attached to my witness statement.

When the work was finished we were pleased because the children had a playroom, but when it rained we had water coming in through the roof panels and under the French windows. Then we noticed water coming in underneath the windows. I contacted Mr Biddulph.

My witness statement has the details of the dates and times. You can see he gave us the 'run around'. In the end, he didn't fix any of the leaks and I had to bring in another builder to correct his shoddy work. I want the defendant to pay for putting it right. We want interest too because we have lost money.

We are not making up the things that went wrong with the conservatory. We asked Gary Kimble to make his statement so that there was a proper record of what went wrong by someone who knows about conservatories. It's in the documents we sent to the defendant and the court.

Oh, I forgot to mention the broken handle on the fanlight window. We had to replace all the handles because we couldn't get a replacement which was the same as the broken one. Mr Biddulph says that he shouldn't have to pay for a whole new set of handles, but we paid for a new modular conservatory that came supplied with all the handles already fitted. It's not my fault that the handle was broken and I don't see why we can't have them all matching since it's what we paid for in the first place. Mr Biddulph can take it up with his suppliers. That's it, really.'

Here is Carol's evidence:

'I'm Carol Clarke and I'm married to Brian. I agree with everything he said just now. I only want to add that I was personally very inconvenienced by the poor quality of Mr Biddulph's work. With Brian working the hours he does, I had to clear up the leaks and clean up the skirting boards. The children couldn't play with their toys in the conservatory when it was leaking and it was a real strain having the toys back in our sitting room. We want interest from George Biddulph to compensate us for the interest we have lost on the money we spent repairing the conservatory. Our Claim Form gives a figure of £18.20, but since then it has gone up. We have also had to compensate Mr Kimble for coming here today so we need the court to order the defendant to pay his expenses. We also had to pay the court £120 for the summons.'

Being cross-examined

After you have given your evidence the defendant is permitted to cross-question you. Lawyers call this 'cross-examination'. The purpose of cross-examination is to cast doubt on the reliability of the evidence of the witness. This can be done by suggesting that:

- memories are faulty;

- evidence is exaggerated;

- evidence is biased and lacks objectivity;

- evidence is inconsistent in various ways by comparing and contrasting previous statements, examining documents and examining exhibits;

- evidence is fabricated;

- there is an alternative explanation of events.

Cross-examination is not an opportunity for a rant against the other side. You should never cross-examine angrily. You should treat the other side with courtesy if you wish to make a good impression on the District Judge. Good cross-questions are focused on the relevant issue in dispute and nothing else. If the defendant has accepted part of your evidence, then only ask about the things that he does not accept.

When asking cross-questions it is better to use closed questions that result in a 'yes' or 'no' answer, but do not be worried if your questions do not result in the defence unravelling. It is rare for cross-examination to cause the defence case to collapse. You really need to focus on flagging up inconsistencies and ambiguities that cast doubt on the defence and make the evidence unreliable.

George Biddulph cross-questions Brian Clarke:

George	It's right that I supplied the conservatory to you at a very good price?
Brian	You told me the supplier had an offer on.
George	Even with one faulty handle, it was an excellent price?

Brian	I'm a store manager, not a builder. I can't say how good the price was. I can only say what we were prepared to pay for a complete conservatory that didn't leak and had a complete set of handles.
George	Yes, you are not a builder. You can't really say what caused the leaks, can you?
Brian	I can say that we didn't have leaks until you built the conservatory.
George	But you cannot really contradict me if I say the roof panels were perfectly well bedded at the time they were put up?
Brian	But they still leaked and when I tried to contact you to find out what was going on you failed to make an appearance.
George	As you are not a builder you cannot say how the water came to be on the floor by the doors?
Brian	But there was a large enough gap for water to come in from outside.
George	You were able to shut the doors, though, weren't you?
Brian	Well, yes.
George	So you can't contradict me if I say there was nothing wrong with the position of the doors, otherwise they would not shut?
Brian	We've got the photos to show what was wrong.
George	It's right that I offered to replace the broken handle?
Brian	Yes, but you wouldn't replace the others so they all matched.
George	Replacing every handle was disproportionate for a standard conservatory of the type installed in your house, surely?
Brian	We paid for a non-leaking conservatory with matching handles.

George	Furthermore, there was nothing wrong with any of the work I carried out?
Brian	I simply don't agree with you. You need only look at the photographs.
George	But the photographs could have been taken anywhere. There is only your word for it that they are of your conservatory.
Brian	The photographs are of our conservatory and I resent you telling the court otherwise.
George	No further questions.
District Judge	Mr Clarke, I have seen the photographs in the album you sent to the court. Photograph number 1 shows you and Mrs Clarke inside the conservatory looking out onto your garden. There is a bare tree a few yards from the French windows. What type is it?
Brian	It's a magnolia tree, Sir.
District Judge	Thank you, Mr Clarke.

After Carol gave her evidence George Biddulph asked her the same question about the window and suggested to her that she was oversensitive about the handles, since she had admitted that the conservatory was essentially a playroom for her children. He also asked her if the children were likely to notice if the handles failed to match. Carol told him that they only wanted what they had paid for.

Examining your witnesses

When the District Judge asks the claimant's witnesses to give evidence he may:

- ask you to take the witness through his evidence and then ask any questions he has at the end; or

- question the witness himself and then let you ask some questions; or

- tell you that he only wishes to hear answers to the questions he asks the witness.

Getting your witnesses to tell their story

As soon as you are ready to take your witness through his witness statement, start by asking your witness to confirm the following:

- His name.

- His address.

- His professional qualifications/number of years' experience in the area of his expertise, if relevant to your claim.

- Ask him to confirm the contents of his witness statement if he has made one. Alternatively, simply ask him to tell the court why he has come to court and then ask him to tell the court about his involvement in your claim. This is usually quite enough to get the witness started on telling his part of the story to the court.

- Ask the witness to deal with any points made by the defence that concern his expertise and/or knowledge of the events.

Ask only open questions

When you are examining your witnesses you may only ask open questions. This means that you cannot ask questions, such as 'It is right that the defendant's work was shoddy, isn't it?' The question implies that there is only one opinion on the matter, but the court is not interested in your opinion; the District Judge wants to know the knowledge/opinion of an unbiased witness. Instead, you have to ask questions such as:

'What did you observe when you examined the defendant's work?'

'What do you think explains the presence of the salts on the interior wall that you referred to in your witness statement?'

'By what means does a competent builder avoid leaks in roof panels?'

'In your opinion, did the defendant adopt this method of working?'

'What do you think accounts for the leak in the roof panels?'

You may ask closed questions when you cross-examine witnesses on the other side.

After your witness has given his evidence, the District Judge will ask his questions unless he decides to let the defendant cross-examine first. After the defendant has finished asking his questions, you have reached the end of your evidence.

The District Judge told Brian and George that he would accept Gary Kimble's witness statement as his evidence-in-chief. Here is how George Biddulph cross-examined Gary Kimble.

George	You and I do all the domestic work in Bays Lea, don't we?
Gary	Yes.
George	You could say we are rivals, really?
Gary	Some might. I just say I do my work for my customers. I haven't the time to worry about what other builders are up to.
George	But that's not right, is it? You came here today because you've been paid to be here.
Gary	I can't leave my work unless I'm paid to be here. I've got a living to earn. But I'm here because I was asked to tell the court about some repairs I carried out on Mr and Mrs Clarke's conservatory. If you're suggesting that my evidence is biased towards them, then you are wrong. I've got my reputation to think of. I never tell customers something needs doing if it doesn't.
George	But you didn't have to replace all the handles on the conservatory, did you?
Gary	That's right. I did tell Mr and Mrs Clarke that they could just replace the broken one because I couldn't get one to match the others, but they

	decided to opt for replacing the lot. It was their choice.
George	So you didn't tell them it was a necessary item of work?
Gary	No, it was their choice.
George	Your estimate puts in £140 for mastic for two roof panels and one window. That price is far too high.
Gary	Not when you consider the time it takes to do the job properly and get a complete seal. My prices are generally higher than some builders in Bays Lea, but then my work is done right the first time.
George	And then there's a price for unnecessary replastering. It could have been treated with inhibitor paint.
Gary	I don't agree. Once there is that much salt contamination the plaster will continue to deteriorate. It was a new conservatory and needed a new plaster surface capable of lasting longer.
George	It isn't right to say that the doors were incorrectly hinged either?
Gary	You can see from photographs 7 and 8 that the doors weren't correctly aligned. You can't explain the gap between the edge of the French windows and the step any other way.
George	But there is an explanation which is that heavy wear and tear will cause the doors to misalign?
Gary	This was a new installation and I wouldn't expect that to happen so early on.
George	All your evidence is given because you have been paid to be here today by the Clarkes.
Gary	I resent that suggestion and, of course, deny it.
George	No further questions.

Closing your case

When all your witnesses have given evidence you can close your case. You do this by saying, 'That is the end of the claimant's evidence. But if the defendant raises any new issues, I should like to answer them.'

The defendant's story

Once the claimant has finished giving his evidence the defendant gives evidence-in-chief. The same rules apply to the defendant's evidence as to the claimant. The defendant may ask the District Judge to accept his statement as his evidence and then just wait to be cross-examined by the claimant. If he has not prepared a statement, then he can simply tell the court his version of events. The District Judge will not permit the claimant to interrupt him when he gives his evidence.

The defendant may represent himself and if he is taking his witnesses through their evidence, he may only ask open questions.

George Biddulph decided to ask the District Judge to accept his witness statement as his evidence.

Questioning the defendant

The same rules apply to cross-examination of the defendant. The purpose of cross-questions is to cast doubt on the defence's evidence by pointing out its weak parts, inconsistency and unreliability. To do this, you need to ask closed questions that require short responses. But be realistic, no matter how carefully you phrase your questions, you will not always get the answer you are looking for. So do not think that by hectoring the witness you will change a negative answer to a positive one. There are two sides to every coin and the defence has its story to tell too. Be prepared to move on once you have made your point.

Here is how Carol cross-questioned George Biddulph:

| Carol | It's right, isn't it, that builders hate returning to the scene of an old job? |

George	It depends.
Carol	You've got my husband's witness statement in front of you, Mr Biddulph. If you look at paragraphs 7 and 8, he tried to contact you eight times and you didn't come round to our house once to look at the faults in your work.
George	Well, I've no record of those calls he says he made.
Carol	Are you saying those calls were never made?
George	No, just I've no record so I couldn't say.
Carol	Mr Biddulph, you knew your work was shoddy and that's why you kept avoiding us?
George	I'm a busy man with a business to run. There was nothing wrong with the work.
Carol	Surely the photographs of our conservatory show otherwise?
George	Except I can't be sure that the photos are of your conservatory. All I can see in the photos are bits of a standard UPVC conservatory. It could be any old conservatory.
Carol	But if you were right, Mr Biddulph, we wouldn't be here?
George	How would I know? People can get some very funny ideas in their heads.
Carol	Well, let's look at some of your ideas. You said in your statement that you don't think that we were entitled to match the handles on the windows and doors?
George	Yes.
Carol	You agree that we paid for a new modular conservatory?
George	Yes.
Carol	So if a handle is broken, you must make sure that the new one matches the rest?

George	Ideally, yes, but not if it means replacing all the other handles. It's just out of proportion to the whole thing. This was just a standard modular conservatory, for a modest house, not a state of the art building.
Carol	Are you saying that 'modest' conservatories are adequate when roof panels leak, windows aren't sealed and French windows are incorrectly hung?
George	I'm saying that there was nothing wrong with my work and the complaints are disproportionate to the price you paid, which was a good one, and what you got.
Carol	Mr Biddulph, you agreed to supply and fit a conservatory that didn't leak and had unbroken fittings. You didn't do so. We're entitled to compensation for the cost of putting your work right.
George	I don't agree.
Carol	No further questions.

What the District Judge will do

When all the evidence has been given and the District Judge is satisfied that he understands all the issues he will give his decision. Some District Judges will give their decision right away. If the issues have been lengthy, he may take a short break to write his decision. However, whatever decision the District Judge makes is based on his assessment of the law, the evidence and his impression of the reliability of the evidence. It is not based on whether he liked one side or the other but on whether the claimant has proved his case. In deciding whether the claimant has proved his case, he must consider whether the claimant has proved his case on the **balance of probability**. This is also known as the 'civil standard of proof'.

District Judge:

1. 'Mr and Mrs Clarke came to court today because they say the defendant failed to correctly fit a modular UPVC conservatory. The work was carried out in November 2005 but soon after the installation Mr and Mrs Clarke allege that:

   - there was water seeping through two roof panels;

   - leaks occurred through the opening of poorly fitted French windows;

   - leaks occurred through the window frame of one window;

   - water and salt saturated plaster beneath that had 'blown';

   - one fanlight window handle was broken.

2. Mr and Mrs Clarke gave evidence that far from being concerned to put matters right, the defendant evaded their many efforts to contact him. Mr Clarke maintains that the defendant then failed to appear as agreed on Saturday 10 December 2005. During his last telephone conversation with Mr Biddulph on 9 January 2006, Mr Clarke gave evidence that he informed Mr Biddulph that he would find another contractor to put right the defects. Mr Kimble of 4Walls Maintenance Company Ltd did just that on 2 February 2006. Mr Biddulph in his evidence maintains that he was unaware of all the efforts Mr Clarke made to contact him and that, in any event, there was nothing wrong with the work carried out. The one concession Mr Biddulph has made is that the fanlight window handle was broken, but he denies that he was obliged to replace all the handles so that they matched and that it would be disproportionate to make him do so given the value and quality of the conservatory.

3. Mr and Mrs Clarke obtained an estimate for this work from Claybourne Building Services Ltd, the defendant, dated 11 October 2005. The estimate appears to set out all the written terms of the contract in that it fully described the work to be carried out, gave the start and completion dates and set out the price and payment terms. Those terms were that 50 per cent of the price should be paid before starting and the rest at the conclusion of the work. I'm satisfied from the witness statements and oral evidence of Brian and Carol Clarke and from the witness statement of Mr Biddulph that those express terms

were the terms of the contract. The contract proceeded in accordance with the estimate and Mr and Mrs Clarke paid for the installation of the conservatory as agreed.

4. What the estimate didn't do was to set out those terms of the contract that are implied by law into contracts for the supply and installation of products, such as the conservatory fitted by the defendant. Implied terms are those terms that are not written down but which the law of contract regards as being implied into a contract by certain Acts of Parliament. The Particulars of Claim on the reverse of the Claim Form make a brief reference to this because it states that the defendant failed to supply a conservatory that was fit for its purpose. The question arises as to whether this contract was one to which the provisions of the Supply of Goods and Services Act 1982, as amended by the Sale and Supply of Goods Act 1994, apply. I consider that they did. Mr Biddulph contracted to supply not just the conservatory but also the professional services of his company in its installation. Section 13 of the Act implies a term that the work will be carried out in a good workmanlike fashion. I consider that Mr Biddulph impliedly warranted the product of his service would be reasonably fit for the purpose since I accept Mr Clarke's evidence that he was aware of the intended purpose of the conservatory.

5. The next question that arises was whether the work to install the conservatory was carried out in a good workmanlike fashion by the employees of Mr Biddulph. In forming my view of that matter, I took account of the evidence of both claimant and defendant. But there was additional assistance from Gary Kimble. Now the defendant takes the view that his evidence is to be disregarded because it's coloured with self-interest. I disagree. I found Gary Kimble to be a careful, reliable witness who brought all his years of experience to bear upon the problem of what had gone wrong with the conservatory. His descriptions of what he observed appeared to me to be accurate and he gave a rational account of his opinion of what had caused the defects in question. I accept his evidence in its entirety. There was additional help from the album of photographs supplied by the claimants. I'm satisfied with their

account of the circumstances in which the photographs were taken. I don't consider that these photographs were taken at another location. I'm satisfied that this conservatory wasn't adequately installed. I consider it was reasonable to expect a new conservatory wouldn't leak or require the remedial work that was carried out.

6. The question of the damages arises. Mr and Mrs Clarke have claimed the cost of engaging Mr Kimble to carry out the remedial work. I've looked carefully at his bill and consider all the sums for curing the various leaks and the replastering and rehanging of the French windows to be recoverable by the claimants. As far as the handles are concerned, I don't consider that the defendant should be liable for replacing them all. I agree that it's disproportionate and award £50 for replacing and fitting just one handle. Consequently, I've adjusted the figures of the claim and daily rate of interest. I award the claimants £981.50, plus interest of £13.23 from the date the sum became due to the date of issue. I award further interest of 21 pence per day from the date of issue, on 13 April 2006 to 4 June 2006, of £10.92. The claimants have won their case and therefore they're entitled to their costs. The costs I'm permitted to award under the rules governing small claims are the costs of issuing the Claim Form of £120 and their witness expenses. I allow £50 to Mr Kimble for those. The defendant must therefore pay the total sum of £1,175.65. I order it to be paid by 5.00pm today. Finally, I should like to thank all the parties for the assistance they all gave to the court in arriving at a decision today.'

What if you disagree with the decision?

You can appeal against the decision of the District Judge to the County Court Judge, but you have to show that the decision was wrong or unjust because of serious procedural error or other irregularity.

CHAPTER 6
Money Claim Online

The good news is that many debtors faced with a County Court Claim Form will respond to it by paying up promptly. The bad news for creditors is that they must go to the effort of issuing the claim in the first place. Chasing debt is time consuming and there are other priorities for your spare time.

If you have embraced the 'third industrial revolution' and have a paperless office system to run your business or domestic affairs, the processes of the County Court may seem rather antiquated. Even with forms available online, only a few courts can accept Claim Forms electronically. The ordinary court user must still print off the Claim Form and send the right number of copies to the court in the post in the usual way. Later the court user will receive documents from the court in the post.

If you wish to maintain a paperless environment, there is an alternative. It is called 'Money Claim Online'. It is a service of the Department for Constitutional Affairs (DCA) and is part of the Court Service. The idea is to permit users access to a system that is totally electronic, from the moment the claim is begun to the time at which the defendant pays you or informs the court that he will defend the claim. This is the system that is used by some debt collection agencies but **it is open to anyone**. To access the service, visit www.moneyclaim.gov.uk or go to www.hmcourts-service.gov.uk and follow the links from there.

You need to have the following to be able to use Money Claim Online:

* Access to a personal computer (Windows or Macintosh).
* Internet connection.

- Microsoft Internet Explorer 4 or 5, Netscape Navigator 4.x or Netscape Communicator 4.x.

- Adobe Acrobat Reader 4.0. The site gives you access to a free download of Acrobat Reader.

How Money Claim Online works

It allows the user to make a claim electronically over the internet against a maximum of two defendants per claim, who have an address in England and Wales where documents can be delivered. Each registered customer is given a unique customer identification and password that allows the user to issue a claim and to follow the progress of the claim through its various stages, from issue to judgment. The progress of any procedure to enforce payment of the judgment debt can be viewed in the same way.

Before you begin using Money Claim Online users are recommended to read through the user's guide. It is easy to follow and answers the questions most likely to arise.

Cases that cannot be started using Money Claim Online are as follows:

- Claims against the Crown
- Claims against children
- Claims by children
- Claims against patients under the Mental Health Act 1983
- Claims by patients under the Mental Health Act 1983
- Claims by a person receiving assistance under the Legal Aid Act 1988
- Claims by a vexatious litigant (see Glossary)
- Claims over £100,000
- Claims against more than two defendants
- Claims where the defendant is being served outside England or Wales
- Claims by a person who does not have a valid credit or debit card
- Claims by persons who qualify for fee remission or exemption

Gaining access to Money Claim Online

The opening page requires the user to identify himself as either a new or an existing customer and to click the relevant arrow. You have to register as a customer of Money Claim Online if you are a new customer. This is done electronically. Users complete information boxes via a series of screens. An example of how they may be answered appears below:

Customer ID	Steven Blake
Password	Camper123
Password confirmation	Camper123
Password reminder question	Mother's maiden name
Favourite music	Pop
Favourite football team	Chelsea
Select a security question	Who is my favourite band?
Password reminder answer	Abba
Type of customer	Individual
Email address	sblake@freebienet.co.uk

Then further boxes for name, address, etc. have to be completed. Once the details are satisfactorily completed, the customer receives a unique customer identification and password. The user then logs in with those details to access the claim service.

When you start to use Money Claim Online, the screen begins by asking you to select the service either to begin a fresh claim or to defend a claim being made against you. If you are making an online claim, you will then gain access to an electronic version of the Claim Form where you can type in the required information online.

The same rules apply to completing the online Claim Form as apply to the paper N1 Form. (Return to chapter 4 for details about completing the Claim Form.) There are exceptions, though:

- You cannot sign the electronic Claim Form. However, the court rules deem the entry of the claimant's name on the online Claim Form to be a signature.

- You must have your credit or debit card handy.

- You must have the details of your claim handy to complete the Claim Form quickly while you are online.

- You will have no more than 24 lines to insert the Particulars of Claim and in total there should be no more than 1,080 characters, letters, numbers, full stops and commas included.

- You can edit what you write as you proceed with the Claim Form, but once you have paid the issue fee to the court you cannot delete or alter your claim. When the form is complete you will be asked to supply credit or debit card details online. The claim will not be issued until the issue fee has been paid.

- All claims issued that use Money Claim Online are started and carry on in the Northampton County Court, unless the defendant resists the claim.

Issuing the Claim Form

This is carried out online as soon as payment by debit or credit card is made. The court fees for issuing online are modestly reduced to take account of the efficiency gains of bulk issue. If the Claim Form is submitted **before 9am** and the court is open, the claim will be issued that day. If it is received after 9am, the claim will be issued the following day that the court is open. Once the fee is paid, the claim number is displayed on the screen. You should print off the number or make a record of it since you will have to quote it on every letter, fax or email to the court.

The system is ideal for multiple issuing of claims. Look at this example.

Clive is a dentist who does a mix of NHS and private work. One Sunday afternoon he took a look at his bills ledger and saw that 20 of them had been unpaid for three months. The usual chasing letters had been sent. Although not one item amounted to more than £300, collectively they amounted to over £2,000. Clive decided to issue Claim Forms for all 20 debts. The first Claim Form Clive completed can be found on the following pages.

Example Claim Form N1

Claim Form

Claimant

Clive Bowley trading as Bowley Dental Services
St George's Terrace
Guildford
Surrey
GU1 5AS

Address for sending documents and payments *(if different)*

Defendant

Miss Heather Dart (d.o.b.18/09/71)
43 Durnsford Road
Guildford
Surrey
GU14 8JR

Particulars of Claim

Fees for dental work.

The claimant is claiming for dental services delivered and materials supplied to the defendant, pursuant to fee note number 05/987 dated 8 March 2005, in the sum of £175 and for interest of £18.12, pursuant to section 09 of the County Courts Act 1984 at the rate of eight per cent per annum from the date of issue and continuing at the daily rate of £0.04 to the date of payment or judgment.

Dated 1 June 2006

The Claimant believes that the facts stated in this claim form are true and I am duly authorised by the claimant to sign this statement

signed *Clive Bowley*

(Claimant)(Claimant's Solicitor)

N1CPC Claim form (04.06) web version

In the

Northampton

County Court

Claim No.	
Issue Date	01/06/06

Court Address

County Court Bulk Centre
4th Floor St. Katharine's House
21-27 St Katharine's Street
Northampton
NN1 2LH

Tel: 01632 496 0563

SEAL

Defendant

Important Note

• You have a limited time in which to reply to this claim form

• Please read all the guidance notes on the back of this form - they set out the time limits and tell you what you can do about the claim

	£
Amount claimed	£193.12
Court fee	£30.00
Solicitor's costs	
Total amount	£223.12

Example Claim Form N1 (continued)

Please read these notes carefully - they will help you decide what to do next.

Court staff can help you complete the reply forms and tell you about court procedures. They cannot give legal advice. If you need legal advice you should contact a solicitor or Citizens Advice Bureau immediately.

Do not ignore this claim form. If you do nothing	Judgment may be entered against you without further notice. This will make it difficult for you to get credit.
Time allowed to reply to this claim	You must respond to this claim form within 14 days of the day of service. The attached forms may be used for that purpose. The day of service is taken as 5 days after the issue date shown overleaf.
If you agree with all of the claim and wish to pay it now	Take or send the money, including any interest and costs, to the claimant. The address for payment is on the front of the claim form. You should ensure that the claimant receives the money within 14 days of the date of service. There is further information on how to pay below.
If you agree with all of the claim and are asking for time to pay.	Complete the admission form (N9A) and send it direct to the claimant (see address on the front of the form to which documents are to be sent). Do not send a copy to the court. Entering an admission may result in judgment being entered against you.
If you admit only part of the claim	Complete the admission form (N9A) and the defence form (N9B) and send them both to the court within 14 days of the date of service.
If you disagree with the claim or if you want to make a claim against the claimant (counterclaim)	You must send either the completed acknowledgment of service form or a defence to the court within 14 days of the date of service. If you send the acknowledgment of service you must send a defence to the court to arrive no later than 28 days from the date of service.

Registration of Judgments: If this claim results in a judgment against you, details will be entered in a public register, the Register of Judgments, Orders and Fines. They will then be passed to credit reference agencies, which will supply them to credit grantors and others seeking information on your financial standing. **This will make it difficult for you to get credit.** A list of credit reference agencies is available from Registry Trust Limited, 173/175 Cleveland Street, London W1T 6QR.

Costs and Interest: Additional costs and interest may be added to the amount claimed on the front of the claim form if judgment is entered against you. If judgment is for £5,000 or more, or is in respect of a debt which attracts contractual or statutory interest for late payment, the claimant may be entitled to further interest.

How to Pay

- payments must be made to the person named at the address for payment box quoting any reference and the court case number
- do not bring or send payments to the court - they will not be accepted
- you should allow at least 4 days for your payments to reach the claimant or his representative
- make sure that you keep records and can account for all payments made. Proof may be required is there is any disagreement. It is not safe to send cash unless you use registered post.
- a leaflet giving further advice about payment can be obtained from any county court
- if you need any further information you should contact the claimant or the claimant's representative

Clive completed another 19 online Claim Forms using the first Claim Form as the template or precedent for the others. Clive only altered the amounts claimed to reflect each individual bill.

Maximum number of Claim Forms

Money Claim Online only permits a claimant to issue a maximum of 100 Claim Forms online in any one session.

Notifying the defendant of the claim

The defendant receives notification through the post of the claim. The defendant receives a Response Pack from the Northampton County Court as he would from any other court.

Date of service

The date of service of the claim is deemed to be five days from the date of its issue. The defendant has 14 days from the date of service to acknowledge service and respond to the claim.

Responding to the claim

The defendant may respond in the usual way and send his response by post to the court. However, the defendant can respond to the claim online by simply visiting the Money Claim Online site and completing the Acknowledgment of Service Form online. The entrance to the site asks the visitor whether he is making or responding to a claim. The defendant may follow the links to acknowledge service of a claim. There is no fee for responding to a claim.

The defendant has the same options in responding to an online claim as to the type received through the post – see chapter 4 for details. The only difference is that he can complete all the Response Pack forms online.

Keeping an eye on your claim

The progress of an online case can be tracked online because there is a record card that can be accessed by inputting your unique customer identification number. A claimant can find out whether a claim has been acknowledged.

Applying for judgment online

If the claim is admitted or partially admitted and the terms are acceptable, a claimant can apply for a judgment online by completing Form N225. The claimant simply selects the 'Judgment start' option. If the defendant ignores the claim, the claimant requests judgment and selects the 'Judgment start' option.

Defendant options	Online claimant response
Pay the claim in full	Complete N225. Select 'Judgment start' option.
Admit the claim but make no payment or offer to pay	Complete Form N225. Select 'Judgment start' option.
Admit the claim and make offer to pay	If the offer is acceptable, complete Form N225. Select 'Judgment start' option.
Part admit claim and make offer to pay	If the offer is acceptable, complete Form N225. Select 'Judgment start' option. If the offer is not acceptable, inform the court within 14 days or the claim will be stayed.
Defend the claim	View the defence online by inputting your unique customer identification number. Check when the claim is transferred to the home court of the defendant.

Make counterclaim online	View counterclaim online by inputting your unique customer identification number. Check out when the claim is transferred to the defendant's home court and then if the counterclaim fee is paid.

Enforcing judgments online

Where no transfer of proceedings has taken place and you have entered judgment you may begin some forms of enforcement online – see chapter 8 for further details.

CHAPTER 7
Getting defensive

The emphasis of this book so far has leaned heavily towards the claimant. It is time to look at things from the perspective of the defendant. However, if you have not already read chapter 4, you should do so before going any further.

Avoid being a defendant

The best way of avoiding the time, expense and stress of defending a claim is not to become embroiled in one in the first place. This is easier said than done, since people are naturally good at becoming involved in conflict. Experienced lawyers are familiar with the situations that lead to litigation. In general, you can expect claims where there is:

- service delivery failure;

- unrealistic expectations of consumers of goods and services;

- failure to communicate effectively;

- failure of service providers to respond adequately to the changing needs and expectations of their consumers.

So, if you have received a Claim Form, consider what lessons it has for you personally or for your business. Do you need to make changes to your practices? Can you settle this claim? Could it be resolved by alternative means or are you happy to take your chance in court where you have no control over the decision?

Usually most people are aware of a dispute before any Claim Form is served on them. As soon as you become aware that you have a dispute that could turn into a claim against you, do seek to negotiate a solution. Many disputes have an element of right on both sides. For further information, visit www.clsdirect.org.uk/legalhelp/leaflet23.jsp.

Do you have a defence?

This is the next matter you need to seriously consider. Certain types of claim do tend to generate predictable defences. Look at the table on the following pages to see what some of these defences are.

Unless you are a lawyer you may find that you cannot always fit your own circumstances into these standard claims and defences. This is the great virtue of the Small Claims Court. It is the District Judge who decides what law is relevant. Therefore, you need to give him as much information as you can about the events surrounding the claim. Although it is for the claimant to prove his claim, the defendant must still show that the claim is not established by mounting a strong defence.

Proving your defence

Even if you do have a defence, proving it is another matter. The court does not examine **the truth** of a claim but **the evidence** to support it. The same is true of defences. If you need witnesses to support your case, will you be able to get them to court? If your defence relies upon paper or electronic records, will you be able to access them or are they lost?

If you are not able to gather the evidence you need to support your defence, you should consider settlement. Even if you have no evidential difficulty, you should still consider settlement to avoid the unnecessary expense of time and money. However, if you consider that you can overcome these hurdles and believe that the claim cannot be resolved amicably, then it is time to look closely at the Response Pack.

Some common defences

Facts	Contract – the law	Defences
A customer is supplied a mobile phone that only works intermittently. The phone company's salesman gave the customer a contract with a finance company to sign, which stated that the agreement would run for three years. The sales agent said that the customer could cancel the agreement after two years. This is the only reason why the customer was prepared to sign it for three years! The finance company states that the customer must pay a penalty of £600 for cancelling early and all the rentals for the last 12 months of the agreement.	Breach of implied terms of the agreement under section 14 of the Sale of Goods Act 1979, as amended by the Sale and Supply of Goods Act 1994. This is because the phone was not of 'satisfactory' quality. The salesman was the agent of the finance company with whom the agreement was made. Breach of warranty that the agreement could be terminated after two years. Penalty clause unfair within the meaning of the Unfair Contracts Terms Act 1977 and the Unfair Terms in Consumer Contracts Regulations 1999.	The finance company is not liable for the statements made by the supplier's salesman. Liability is specifically excluded under the terms of the agreement. Clauses excluding liability are fair under the Unfair Terms in Consumer Contracts Regulations 1999 because the finance company has no expertise in the goods themselves. They have expertise in the provision of finance. The consumer can begin action for breach of warranty of authority against the salesman.

Some common defences (continued)

Facts	Contract – the law	Defences
		Penalty is a fair reflection of the costs of repossessing the goods and selling them on. The goods cannot be hired out because customers only want up-to-date models.
A 'pre-owned' car turns out to be a wreck.	Breach of implied terms of contract pursuant to sections 13 and 14 of the Sale of Goods Act 1979, as amended by the Sale and Supply of Goods Act 1994 that the car would be of satisfactory quality for a car of its age and type and fit for the purpose of being driven.	'Rescission' not possible because the customer has left it too late and adopted the vehicle by using it and getting it repaired. The car was not returned immediately, therefore only damages are recoverable and the car's market value has slumped since the sale.

Some common defences (continued)

Facts	Contract – the law	Defences
A small business purchases a new computer to keep the accounts, PAYE records for five employees and the book-keeping ledgers and correspondence. The computer produced software does not work as it should and the computer keeps crashing. The book-keeper has to spend time sorting it out.	Breach of implied terms that that the software would be of satisfactory quality and fit for its purpose, pursuant to sections 13 and 14 of the Sale of Goods Act 1979, as amended by the Sale and Supply of Goods Act 1994.	The software was of satisfactory quality and the designers did not guarantee a particular result. No evidence was provided to show the connection between the computer crashing and the software failure. Limitation clause in terms of contract limited liability to £250. This was fair under the Unfair Contracts Terms Act 1977.
A builder installs a new kitchen that costs £11,000. After the installation is complete, the householder notices that: **1.** the door of the 'built-in' refrigerator does not fit properly	Breach of implied terms that that the kitchen would be of satisfactory quality and fit for its purpose, pursuant to sections 13 and 14 of the Sale of Goods Act 1979, as amended by the Sale and Supply of Goods Act 1994.	The builder's terms and conditions limited the liability of the builder to replacement only of the faulty appliances, which the builder has offered to do.

Some common defences (continued)

Facts	Contract – the law	Defences
because it juts out from the line of the rest of the kitchen cupboard units; 2. the extractor fan does not work because the unit is broken; 3. one of the wall cupboard doors does not match the colour of the rest of the units; 4. the seal on the sink leaks, the freezer ices up very quickly and when it does the door will not shut; 5. one of the two plinth heaters has failed.	Breach of implied term of the contract to carry out the work with due care and skill by section 13 of the Supply of Goods and Services Act 1982, as amended by the Sale and Supply of Goods Act 1994. Breach of section 4(2) of the Sale and Supply of Goods and Services Act 1982 in that the appliances supplied were not of satisfactory quality.	The builder did not guarantee an exact colour match of the units to the dresser and warned the customer that he could only use his best endeavours to match the units to the dresser prior to starting work.
A motor car is taken to a garage to be repaired. When the owner collects it he notices that the hub caps are missing and the satellite navigation system has been removed. The garage insists that it was locked up	Breach of 'bailment'. The garage was under a duty to look after the vehicle while it was being repaired and to ensure that it was locked away securely when unattended. Negligent omission to ensure that the	The garage's standard terms and conditions of trading made the vehicle owner responsible for removing valuable items from the car prior to it

Some common defences (continued)

Facts	Contract – the law	Defences
while it was with them and will not pay for the missing items.	premises was secure against theft.	being left at the garage. The garage is not liable for replacing new ones for old ones but like for like. The hub caps were, like the car, in poor condition.
Three-piece suite reupholstering poorly executed. Fabric sagging on the cushions and the piping on the cushions does not line up properly with the piping on the back cushions of the sofa.	Breach of implied term of the contract to carry out the work with due care and skill by section 13 of the Supply of Goods and Services Act 1982, as amended by the Sale and Supply of Goods Act 1994.	Liability of the upholsterer limited by its terms and conditions to work being done again. The upholsterer had agreed to do this. Limitation of liability not unfair since the upholsterer had warned the customer that the fabric she had chosen was likely to result in a less than perfect look when combined with natural material filling in the cushions.

Dealing with the Response Pack

When a claim is served on you by the court you will receive the following documents:

- N1 Claim Form
- N1C Notes for replying to the Claim Form
- Response Pack which contains:
  - N9 Acknowledgment of Service Form
  - N9A Admission Form for Specified Amount
  - N9B Defence/Counterclaim for Specified Amount
  - N1C Notes for Defendant on Replying to a Claim Form

  or

  - N9 Acknowledgment of Service Form
  - N9C Admission for Unspecified Amount and Non-Money Claim
  - N9D Defence/Counterclaim for Unspecified Amount and Non-Money Claim
  - N1C Notes for Defendant on Replying to a Claim Form

If the Claim Form arrived by post, you need to look at the envelope in which the Claim Form arrived. It will have a postmark showing the date of posting. The date of service of the claim is deemed by the courts to be the second day after posting, so do not throw away the envelope. It is the record of the date of posting and therefore tells you the date of service. It may become important if, for a genuine reason, you were unaware of the claim. We will return to this problem later. But it is also very important because you must reply to the Claim Form **within 14 days of the date of service**. If you do not, the claimant can enter judgment against you.

Acknowledging service

Form N9, which should be at the top of the Response Pack, contains an

Acknowledgment of Service Form. If you are defending the claim, you should complete it right away and send it to the court as soon as possible. Remember to keep a completed copy for your own records. Sending the Acknowledgment of Service Form to the court also has the fortunate effect of giving you longer to consider your defence. (You have 28 days from the service of the Claim Form to file your defence with the court.) Remember that you must complete all parts of the form, including the part requesting your date of birth. If you do not, then the court will refuse to file the acknowledgment and the claimant will be able to enter judgment in default 14 days after the service of the Claim Form.

Considering the claim

Next, you need to carefully study the Claim Form to see what the allegations are and decide how you are going to respond. You have the choices referred to in chapter 4:

- Pay the amount claimed, and the issue fee.

- Admit you owe all or part of the claim, make an offer of payment and/or ask the court for time to pay.

- Defend the claim.

Whether you admit the claim or defend it, you **must respond** to the claim **within 14 days of the date of service** of the claim. If you do nothing, the claimant will be entitled to enter **judgment in default** against you. Once the claimant has a judgment he will also be able to instruct the bailiff to enter your home or business premises to seize any goods that have a resale value. Once the bailiff has your chattels, he is entitled to sell them and take a cut of the sale price to satisfy his fees and then the claimant's judgment.

Admitting the claim

Complete Form N9A and send the payment with the form to **the claimant**. Do **not** send money to the court. Make sure that the payment includes the sum claimed, any interest claimed and the court costs. If you are paying by cheque, keep a photocopy of it. Also, keep proof that you have posted the letter containing Form N9A and the cheque, since claimants are used to the phrase, 'It's in the post' and are disinclined to believe it. Send another photocopy of the cheque to the court with your completed reply forms. You must do this **within 14 days** of the date of service.

Admitting <u>all</u> the claim and asking for time to pay

Complete Form N9A **within 14 days** of the service of the Claim Form and ask the claimant to accept staged payments of a fixed amount per month over a period of time. Be realistic about what you can pay and provide the claimant with as much information as is requested on your income and expenses. A claimant is more likely to accept your offer if full information is given and the payments are spread out over a short period of time. Claimants are unlikely to agree to payments that stretch out over a couple of years. Whether or not your offer is accepted, the claimant will probably request the court to enter judgment against you. If the claimant does not accept your offer to pay, the court will fix the payments you must make. It is wise to keep full records and proof of the payments you make. If you fail to make one payment, the claimant can request the bailiff to seize your goods.

Admitting <u>part</u> of the claim and asking for time to pay

Complete Form N9A and Form N9B and return it to the court **within 14 days** of the date of service of the Claim Form. This does not guarantee that the claimant will accept your offer. If the claimant does accept your offer, it is likely that the claimant will request the court to enter judgment against you. This is to encourage defendants to make the payments ordered by the courts and to ensure that the bailiff can seize your goods should you fail to do so. If your part admission is not accepted, the court will treat the claim as a defended one. Remember that defendants who are individuals must provide their date of birth on the Acknowledgment of Service Form or Admission Form or Defence and Counterclaim. This is to ensure that the bailiffs identify the debtor correctly when they enforce judgments.

Disputing the jurisdiction of the court

If you consider that the court does not have the power to consider the claim, you must inform the court. To do this, find 'Tick the appropriate box' on the Acknowledgment of Service Form. The circumstances in which you might be disputing the jurisdiction of the court vary. In the Small Claims Court it may arise if a written contract, such as a standard form building contract, contains an arbitration clause or an adjudication clause. If you do wish the claim to proceed via adjudication or arbitration, you must inform the court before you file your defence. The court will treat you as having waived the right to dispute its jurisdiction if you do not tick the box at number 3 on the Acknowledgment of Service Form. You will also have to complete Form N244 setting out why the court should not hear the case.

Disputing a claim

If you have decided that the claimant is not entitled to the sum claimed, complete Form N9B. You will need to send it to the court **within 14 days** of the date of service. If you have sent the Acknowledgment of Service Form to the court, you will have 28 days from service of the claim to send your N9 Defence Form to the court. The details of the defence should be inserted into part 3 in the box headed 'Defence'. If you have a claim of your own to make against the claimant, you can insert the details in box 4. This is called a 'counterclaim'.

As it is treated as a claim in its own right, you will have to pay a fee to the court before you can proceed with it. The fee is on the same scale as the claim fees (see chapter 1). Once the court has received the defendant's response, it sends copies of the relevant forms to the claimant and then sends you and the claimant an Allocation Questionnaire in Form N149. If you do not pay the court fee, you will be unable to proceed with your counterclaim.

What if the court enters judgment in default against me?

The County Court system is designed to work by making defendants aware of claims so that they have an opportunity to respond to them. However, the rules recognise that from time to time judgment in default may be entered against a defendant who is unaware of the claim. If so, the defendant may apply to set aside judgment and obtain permission to defend the claim. To make the application, you need to complete Form N244. It can be downloaded from www.hmcourts-service.gov.uk or you can get it from a County Court office. You should complete it as follows:

- **Box underneath 'Application Notice'**

  There are six questions in this box. The first asks how you want your application to be dealt with. If you opt for a hearing, you will have to attend court to speak with the District Judge. This has the distinct advantage that you will be able to explain personally to him how you came to have a judgment entered against you. A District Judge is more inclined to grant an application to set aside judgment where the person concerned appears. If you are not a lawyer, this is probably your best option.

  Question 2 requires you to say how long the application will take. This kind of application is generally disposed of quickly, especially if the claimant does not have a lawyer to represent him. In this case you should probably insert between 15 and 30 minutes. You can also telephone the court office to see how long the court likes to set aside for these types of application.

- **Part A**

  Insert your name and delete 'the claimant'. After 'intend to apply for an order that' insert 'the judgment in default dated [*judgment date*] be set aside and the defendant given leave to defend'. Underneath 'because' insert that the claim did not come to the attention of the defendant because [*insert reasons*].

- **Part B**

  The three options in Part B require you to tick one of the boxes. It is probably best to tick 'evidence in Part C in support of my application'.

- **Part C**

  This is the part where you can fully set out all the circumstances in which the judgment was entered. To be successful, you must provide as much detailed evidence as possible to support:

  - what you say about the service of the claim; and

  - the strength of your defence.

  If you did not receive the claim and Response Pack, then you can say why that was. Sometimes defendants may have been away for extended periods of time. If this has happened, the court will require strong evidence to support what you say. It will need to see evidence of travel to and from the place you went to.

  At other times judgment in default may have been entered because the Claim Form was not delivered to the correct address. But, again, the court will need strong evidence that it was not delivered before it will set aside judgment. It will also need to know what the defence to the claim is. The court will not set aside judgment unless there is a serious likelihood that you will defend successfully. You should complete Form N9B or N9D and attach it to the application form.

- **The statement of truth**

  This must be signed or the application cannot proceed.

When the application form is completed send:

- two copies to the court;

- one copy for each defendant; and

- the correct fee.

The court will not hear the application unless you have paid the correct court fee. As the fees change regularly you need to check the amount either with the court or at the Court Service website. The court will then send one sealed copy of the application to the defendant, keep one sealed copy for its file and give or send you one sealed copy.

Now, look at the example below to see how the process of setting aside judgment works:

Grace and her elderly mother decided to have a satellite dish installed by TV Dish Ltd on a three-month trial. The service was provided by Stellar Plc. After two months Grace and her mother decided that they no longer wanted the service.

As Grace and her mother were due to fly to Canada to visit relatives she wrote and explained that they would be leaving the country for a couple of months. Grace asked Stellar to collect the equipment. They did not do so. When Grace and her mother returned they found a letter from the bulk claims centre at Northampton County Court informing them that judgment in default had been issued against them. Grace immediately telephoned the court. An officer of the court said that she would have to apply to set aside judgment. Grace also tried to telephone Stellar but the automatic answering service did not have an option to speak to a real person other than one in the sales department. The Sales Manager said she should write to the customer service department and refused to put her in telephone contact with them. Grace made an application to set aside judgment on using Form N244. Her form can be found on the following pages.

The District Judge did set aside judgment on the grounds that it had not come to the attention of the defendants and that they should be allowed to defend the claim. Before the trial date Grace spoke to the claimant over the telephone and they agreed to withdraw the claim.

How do I write a defence?

A defence should be tackled in the same way as a claim. You need to set out the details on Form N9B or D, succinctly and with a sufficient amount of detail. A bare denial of the claim is not adequate, for example 'The claim is denied'. If you do not spell out why the claim is wrong, the District Judge will be entitled to strike out the defence and permit the claimant to enter judgment.

The defence should answer each allegation made by the claimant. If it does not, then the court will conclude that you have accepted what the claimant states; for example, the claimant states in Form N1 that the defendant agreed to pay for upholstering a sofa in blue cambric cloth at £20.99 per metre. If the defendant had actually agreed to pay for pink 'Dralon' at

Example Application Notice Form N244

Application Notice	In the
You should provide this information for listing the application	CARDIFF COUNTY COURT

1. How do you wish to have your application dealt with	

a) at a hearing? ☑ } complete all questions below
b) at a telephone conference? ☐
c) without a hearing? ☐ complete Qs 5 and 6 below

Claim no.	CD067845
Warrant no. (if applicable)	
Claimant (including ref.)	Stellar Plc

2. Give a time estimate for the hearing/conference
_____ (hours) 30 (mins)

3. Is this agreed by all parties? ☐ Yes ☑ No

4. Give dates of any trial period or fixed trial date _____

Defendant(s) (including ref.)	Gwyneth Rees Grace Rees

5. Level of judge District Judge
6. Parties to be served Defendant

Date	3 March 2006

Note You must complete Parts A and B, and Part C if applicable. Send any relevant fee and the completed application to the court with any draft order, witness statement or other evidence; and sufficient copies for service on each respondent.

Part A

1. Enter your full name, or name of solicitor

I (We)[1] Gwyneth Rees
Grace Rees

(on behalf of)(the claimant)(the defendant)

2. State clearly what order you are seeking and if possible attach a draft

intend to apply for an order (a draft of which is attached) that[2]

the judgment entered against us on 27 February 2006 be set aside

3. Briefly set out why you are seeking the order. Include the material facts on which you rely, identifying any rule or statutory provision

because[3]

the Claim Form did not come to our attention and we wish to dispute the claim

Part B

I (We) wish to rely on. tick one box

the attached (witness statement)(affidavit) ☐   my statement of case ☐

4. If you are not already a party to the proceedings, you must provide an address for service of documents

evidence in Part C in support of my application ☑

Signed *Gwyneth Rees   Grace Rees*

(Applicant)('s Solicitor)('s litigation friend)

Position or office held _____
(if signing on behalf of firm or company)

Address to which documents about this claim should be sent (including reference if appropriate)[4]

23 Tennyson Road Roath Cardiff		if applicable
	fax no.	
	DX no.	
Tel. no. 01632 496 0637 Postcode CF24 6DX	e-mail	reesg@bestprice.com

The court office at

is open from 10am to 4pm Monday to Friday. When corresponding with the court please address forms or letters to the Court Manager and quote the claim number.

Example Application Notice Form N244 (continued)

Part C

Claim No. CD067845

I (We) wish to rely on the following evidence in support of this application:

In October 2005 my mother, Mrs Gwyneth Rees, and I agreed to take a satellite dish for a three-month trial period. The system came from TV Dish Limited, the supplier. Their saleswoman gave me an agreement to sign with the claimant, Stellar Plc. The saleswoman told me that if we decided we would like the satellite service at the end of the trial period, the agreement would just carry on for three years. I asked her what we should do if we didn't want the system and she told me that I should telephone the company and ask them to remove the system. There would be nothing to pay. I attach a copy of the agreement with Stellar Plc.

By the end of October 2005 my mother and I concluded we were unlikely to gain much from satellite TV and so I telephoned Stellar Plc and asked them to remove the system. I was assured an engineer would come and remove it the following week. I informed the person to whom I spoke that we would be leaving the country on 14 December 2005 and that we would be away after that for three or four months. I was assured it would be. But because I wasn't confident I also wrote a letter to confirm the conversation dated 30 November 2005. I attach a copy of that letter. No one called to collect the equipment even though I telephoned again on 5 December and again on 12 December. We left the country on 14 December and returned on 2 March 2006. I attach photocopies of our flight confirmations.

On our return I was shocked to find a Claim Form from Stellar Plc and notification of judgment against us. I immediately contacted the court but was told that I couldn't defend until I had set judgment aside.

I request the court to set aside judgment. We didn't receive notification of the claim because we were away and I believe we have a defence to it anyway. We didn't sign up to any agreement and for Stellar Plc to say that we confirmed a three-year agreement by not notifying them is sharp practice and unfair. I did everything I could to tell them that we didn't want their product, which they have still not removed.

Statement of Truth

*(I believe) *(The applicant believes) that the facts stated in Part C are true
*delete as appropriate

Signed   *Gwyneth Rees   Grace Rees*

(Applicant)('s Solicitor)('s litigation friend)

Position or office held

(if signing on behalf of firm or company)

Date   3 March 2006

£6.99 per metre, the defendant will have to take this up in the defence. If he does not, the court will conclude that the claimant was correct.

It is not difficult to ensure that you answer the claimant. All you have to do is look at the Particulars of Claim on Form N1 and decide what positive assertions the claimant is making and decide whether you agree with them. Look at the Particulars of Claim set out on page 2 of Form N1 by the claimant, Clever Kitchens Ltd, on the following page.

The Particulars of Claim make the following positive statements that appear in the left column of the table below. The defence appears in the right column.

Claim statement	Defence to statement
Claim is for building services	Agreed.
A pine 'Quaker' kitchen was supplied to the defendant	Agreed.
Materials were supplied to the defendant	Agreed.
£2,500 remains unpaid	Agreed.
The claimant is entitled to £2,500	Denied as the installation of the kitchen was defective for the following reasons: • The plinth heaters did not work. • The fridge door was not properly hung and the seal was torn and the whole door has to be replaced. • The microwave oven failed and needs replacing. • The mastic seal around the sink leaked and must be renewed. • The claimant warranted the colour of the wall cupboards would match the existing pine dresser but they did not. It will cost the defendant £2,500 to put the

Example Particulars of Claim 1

	Claim No.	

Does, or will, your claim include any issues under the Human Rights Act 1998? ☐ Yes ☑ No

Particulars of Claim (attached)(to follow)

The claimant is claiming for building services delivered and materials supplied to the defendant, pursuant to Invoice Number 06/679, dated 27 March 2006, in the sum of £2,500, being the balance of sums due for the installation of a pine 'Quaker' kitchen and for interest of £20.35 pursuant to section 69 of the County Courts Act 1984 at the rate of eight per cent per annum from the due date to the date of issue and continuing at the daily rate of £0.55 to the date of payment or judgment.

Dated 2 May 2006

Statement of Truth
*(I believe)(The Claimant believes) that the facts stated in these particulars of claim are true.
* I am duly authorised by the claimant to sign this statement

Full name _____

Name of claimant's solicitor's firm _____

signed _____ position or office held _____

*(Claimant)(Litigation friend)(Claimant's solicitor)   (if signing on behalf of firm or company)

*delete as appropriate

Clever Kitchens Limited
227 Bellingham Road
London N11 9AG

Kitchens@clkworld.com

Claimant's or claimant's solicitor's address to which documents or payments should be sent if different from overleaf including (if appropriate) details of DX, fax or e-mail.

	defective work right and replace the faulty appliances.
	• The worktop is gouged and damaged and needs replacing.
The claimant is entitled to interest on the sum claimed	Denied as the claimant is not entitled to the sum claimed.

The defendant agrees the first four statements. Therefore, he need only deny the two statements in the last two rows. In making his denial, the defendant positively asserts his defence.

'The defendant denies the claimant is entitled to £2,500 since the installation of the kitchen was defective in that the plinth heaters did not work, the fridge door was not properly hung and the seal was torn and the whole door needs replacing. The microwave oven failed and has to be replaced, the mastic seal around the sink leaks and the sink will have to be removed and resealed. The claimant promised that the colour of the wall cupboards would match the existing pine dresser, but they do not. It will cost £2,500 to put the defective work right and replace the faulty appliances. As the claimant is not entitled to the sum claimed it follows that the claimant is not entitled to the interest on it.'

An example of the Particulars of Claim on Form N1 for a personal injury claim can be found on the following page.

Here is the defence to such a claim that would appear in box 1 of Form N9D:

'The claimant was present at my home office on 21 February 2005 and I accept that he suffered the injuries set out in the medical reports attached to the Claim Form, but I deny that his accident was as a result of my negligence. The filing cabinet drawer was stuck and I verbally warned the claimant twice not to enter my office until I had managed to shut it again. The claimant ignored my warning and then failed to look sufficiently well to avoid the hazard of the filing cabinet. The claimant is responsible for his own injuries. If the claimant has suffered the losses he claims, I am not legally responsible for them, nor for paying him interest, since the claimant is the author of his own misfortune.'

Example Particulars of Claim 2

	Claim No.	01/

Does, or will, your claim include any issues under the Human Rights Act 1998? ☐ Yes ☑ No

Particulars of Claim (attached)(to follow)

On 21 February 2005 the claimant, who was born on 29 November 1971, was at the defendant's premises when he tripped over a filing cabinet drawer that had been negligently left open and suffered personal injury, loss and damage. Details of the claimant's injuries are in the attached medical reports and details of the claimant's losses are in the attached schedule of losses.

The claimant claims:

(1) General damages limited to £1,000 for personal injuries, together with interest from 21 February to the date of judgment, as set out on the attached schedule, under s.69 of the County Courts Act 1984;

(2) Special damages of £500 for loss of earnings and travel expenses together with interest, as set out on the attached schedule, under s.69 of the County Courts Act 1984.

Statement of Truth
*(I believe)(The Claimant believes) that the facts stated in these particulars of claim are true.
* I am duly authorised by the claimant to sign this statement

Full name _____

Name of claimant's solicitor's firm _____

signed _____ position or office held_____
*(Claimant)(Litigation friend)(Claimant's solicitor)   (if signing on behalf of firm or company)
*delete as appropriate

Claimant's or claimant's solicitor's address to which documents or payments should be sent if different from overleaf including (if appropriate) details of DX, fax or e-mail.

Counterclaims

A counterclaim is a claim brought against the claimant by the defendant. It usually arises out of the same facts that concern the claim. You can see how this can happen by looking at the personal injury claim at page 160. Here is the counterclaim that was inserted into box 2 of Form N9D:

'The claimant's own negligence in tripping over the filing cabinet drawer referred to caused my Meissen vase, on top of the filing cabinet, to fall to the floor. The vase worth £2,000 was irreparably broken. I attach a copy of the sales receipt from 'Anthony Antiques' to this form. I claim £2,000 plus costs of £120 plus interest under section 69 of the County Courts Act 1984 from 21 February 2005 to the date of judgment on my counterclaim.'

A 'counterclaim' is a claim

The court regards a counterclaim as a claim in its own right. If the defendant were to admit the claim, then you would still be able to continue with your counterclaim. Consequently, the court also expects you to pay a fee for its services in administering it. If you do not pay the fee when you send your defence and counterclaim to the court, it will send you a letter giving you seven days to do so. If you still fail to pay the fee, the court will strike out the counterclaim. The amount of the fee is calculated in the same way as for claims. If the claim began using Money Claim Online, and the court fee for the counterclaim is not paid, the County Court Bulk Centre in Northampton will transfer the claim to the defendant's home court. The home court will then warn you to pay the fee.

Statement of truth

Remember that the statement of truth must be signed in the relevant boxes of Forms N9B and D.

What happens if you defend successfully

If you win the trial, you are entitled to claim the following:

- Witness expenses, if any
- Compensation for loss of earnings or holiday entitlement

Winning the counterclaim

If the claimant fails to win the claim but you win the counterclaim, then you are entitled to:

- judgment on the counterclaim;
- the compensation you sought in the counterclaim;
- your issue fee for the counterclaim;
- witness expenses, if any;
- compensation for loss of earnings or holiday entitlement.

You can enforce judgment on a counterclaim in the same way as a claim.

What if the claimant wins the claim and you win the counterclaim

The District Judge may set off the claim against the counterclaim and award the costs to the overall 'winner'. So if the successful claim was £600 but the successful counterclaim was £900, the District Judge could order the claimant to pay the defendant's costs. Many District Judges, however, would simply make no order for costs. This would mean that the claimant and defendant would bear their own costs.

CHAPTER 8

Getting your money out of the debtor

Winning your claim can be the much shorter part of the recovery of your debt. It is one thing to win a judgment, but it is another thing altogether to have it paid. The good news is that most judgments are paid because people are afraid of losing a good credit rating and being refused future credit. But if your debtor does not take the court's judgment seriously, you can take one or more of the following steps:

- Apply for a warrant of execution.

- Apply for an order that the debtor attends court so he can be examined as to his means to pay the debt.

- Apply for a charging order against his property.

- Apply for an attachment of earnings order.

- Apply for a third party debt order.

- Apply for an order of bankruptcy.

- Apply for a winding up order against a company.

However, before you take any of these steps you should also make some checks against the defendant to see if he has any unsatisfied judgments or other orders outstanding against him. This applies even if you made those checks before you started your claim. A debtor may have admitted a number of other claims and lost court cases since your claim began.

What if your debtor could afford to pay more than the court has ordered

If the debtor has other means to pay which he has not revealed to the court in his Form N9A, you can ask the court for an order that he pay by larger instalments or even the full amount. To do this, you need to complete Form N244. It is available at www.hmcourts-service.gov.uk.

Warrant of execution

This is an order by which the court permits the bailiff to go to the debtor's property to remove his personal possessions and sell them. The sale usually takes place at an auction and the bailiff will sell the goods to the highest bidder. When the bailiff has collected the money from the sale he deducts his own fees. Whatever is left is then used to pay the debt. If anything is left after the debt is paid off, it is returned to the debtor.

To obtain the order you must complete a Request for Warrant of Execution Form (N323). You can download it from the Court Service website or obtain one from your local court office. Completing the form is simple but when you reach box 4(A) 'Balance due at date of this request', do make sure that you put the correct figure in. The correct figure appears on the judgment form you received, plus any interest and costs ordered by the court. If you have received any payment from the debtor, you must deduct it from the figure that goes in this box. If your debtor has sent you a cheque but it has not cleared by the time you apply for the warrant, you cannot give credit for it.

At 4(B) 'Amount for which warrant to issue', put in the figure you inserted at A above. You will need to check the issue fee with the court, since its fees are regularly revised. The section at the end of the form asking for contact details is very important. It requests you to give any other information that will help the bailiff succeed in seizing the debtor's possessions. If, for example, you know the debtor keeps a valuable car but it is parked outside his mother's house, then you need to give the bailiff the relevant details.

Once the form is complete you will need:

Request for Warrant of Execution Form N323

Request for Warrant of Execution
to be completed and signed by the claimant or his solicitor and sent to the court with the appropriate fee

1 Claimant's name and address

Lawrence Harding trading as Harding Domestic Roofing
Ondine Drive
Milton Keynes
MK16 2PW

In the
BEDFORD COUNTY COURT
County Court

Claim Number BDF066523

2 Name and address for service and payment (if different from above) Ref/Tel No.

for court use only
Warrant no.

Issue date:

Warrant applied for at   o'clock

3 Defendant's name and address

Jason Gornal (d.o.b. 12.02.64) t/a Jason's Gym
6 Fennel Lane
Bedford
MK43 6GL

Foreign court code/name:

4 Warrant details

(A) Balance due at date of this request	£1,099.36
(B) Amount for which warrant to issue	
Issue fee	£35.00
Solicitor's costs	
Land Registry fee	
TOTAL	£1,134.36

If the amount of the warrant at (B) is less than the balance at (A), the sum due after the warrant is paid will be

I certify that the whole or part of any instalments due under the judgment or order have not been paid and the balance now due is as shown

Signed   *Lawrence Harding*

Claimant (Claimant's solicitor)

Dated 31 March 2006

IMPORTANT
You must inform the court immediately of any payments you receive after you have sent this request to the court

You should provide a contact number so that the bailiff can speak to you if he/she needs to:

Daytime phone number: 01632 573 271   Evening phone number (if possible): 07700 900 630

Contact name (where appropriate):

Defendant's phone number (if known): 01632 549 347

If you have any other information which may help the bailiff or if you have reason to believe that the bailiff may encounter any difficulties you should write it below.

The defendant is the owner of a highly successful gymnasium which is open between 0600 and 2300, every day other than bank holidays. It is fitted out with the latest equipment and is reputed to have been kitted out entirely for cash.

N323 -w5- Request for warrant of execution (4.99)   *Produced on behalf of The Court Service*

- One copy for the court records
- One copy for the debtor
- One copy for the bailiff
- One copy for your records

When you send the forms to the court do make sure that you include the issue fee or the court will not issue the request to the bailiff.

An example of Form N323 can be found on the previous page. In this case, the information on the form helped the bailiff considerably. The bailiff went to the gym and took possession of all the equipment. The debtor paid the bailiff before lunchtime!

Debtor examination

It is not always clear whether the debtor has any assets. One way to find out is to bring the defendant to court to answer questions. Complete Form N316. Make sure that you send the court three copies of the form together with the issue fee. If you do not send the fee, the court will not issue the request. You will need to check the amount of the fee as the fees are regularly revised. Once the request form has been issued by the court, the court bailiff will then serve the order to attend. The debtor is entitled to ask you to send him enough money to cover his travel expenses to court.

An officer of the court conducts the oral examination of the debtor. The questions are on a standard form used by the court. The debtor will have to produce documents to prove his income and expenditure. The court officer makes a record of the examination of the debtor. The information can be helpful in deciding how to enforce the debt if, for example, it reveals that the debtor owns a property that has only a small mortgage or he has a well-paid job and few expenses. An example of a request for an oral examination of a debtor can be found on the following pages.

Leaflet EX324 is available at County Court offices and at www.hmcourts-service.gov.uk. It gives guidance on obtaining information from a judgment debtor.

Application for Order that Debtor Attend Court for Questioning Form N316

Application for order that debtor attend court for questioning

In the

Claim No.

Appn. No.

Claimant

Defendant

The [claimant] [defendant] ('the judgment creditor') applies for an order that the [defendant] [claimant] ('the judgment debtor') attend court to provide information about the judgment debtor's means and any other information needed to enforce the judgment or order given on   20 [by the   in claim no.   ].

1. Judgment debtor

The judgment debtor is
whose address is

Postcode

2. Judgment debt or order

[The judgment or order required the judgment debtor to pay £   (including any costs and interest). The amount now owing is £   [which includes further interest payable on the judgment debt]].

[The judgment or order required the judgment debtor to

]

Note:

Questioning and documents

Questioning will be by a court officer unless a judge agrees there are compelling reasons for questioning to take place before a judge. Normally the court officer will ask the questions set out in Form EX140 and the judgment debtor will be told to produce all relevant documents including:

- pay slips
- bank statements
- building society books
- share certificates
- rent book

- mortgage statement
- hire purchase and similar agreements
- court orders
- any other outstanding bills
- electricity, gas, water and council tax bills for the past year.

and in the case of a business

- bills owed to it
- 2 years' accounts
- current management accounts.

Complete sections 3, 4 and 5 only if applicable.
The statement of truth overleaf must be completed.

N316 Application for order that debtor attend court for questioning (03.02)   *Printed on behalf of The Court Service*

Application for Order that Debtor Attend Court for Questioning Form N316 (continued)

3. [Attached is a list of questions which the judgment creditor wishes the court officer to ask the judgment debtor in addition to those in Form EX140.]

4. [Attached is a list of documents which the judgment creditor wishes the judgment debtor to be ordered to produce in addition to those listed in the note above.]

5. [The judgment creditor requests that the judgment debtor be questioned by the judgment creditor before a judge. The reason for this request is

]

Statement of Truth

*(I believe)(The judgment creditor believes) that the facts stated in this application form are true.
* I am duly authorised by the judgment creditor to sign this statement.

signed _____ date _____

(Judgment creditor)(Litigation friend(where judgment creditor is a child or a patient)*)(Judgment creditor's solicitor)
*delete as appropriate

Full name _____

Name of judgment creditor's solicitor's firm _____

position or office held _____
 (if signing on behalf of firm or company)

Judgment creditor's or judgment creditor's solicitor's address to which documents should be sent.		if applicable	
		Ref. no.	
		fax no.	
		DX no.	
	Postcode		
Tel. no.		e-mail	

Attachment of earnings order

As the name implies, the order permits the creditor to attach his debt to the debtor's regular income. The order is obtained by completing a Request for Attachment of Earnings Form (N337). You need to send two copies to the court together with the issue fee. If the issue fee is not sent, the request is not issued. You need to check the amount of the fee with the court. Once the request is issued the court sends the debtor's employer a Request for Statement of Earnings requiring the employer to give detailed information on the debtor's earnings. If the court does grant the order, it will be transferred to the County Court Bulk Centre in Northampton and the employer will be obliged to send a portion of the debtor's earnings to the bulk centre. The payment of all attachment of earnings payments occurs at the County Court Bulk Centre in Northampton via Centralised Attachment of Earnings Payments (CAPS). The system has been modified so that deductions from the employee's earnings can be transferred via the BACS system. The additional administrative burden for the employer is unlikely to enhance the debtor's career prospects. For this reason some debtors will pay up to avoid embarrassment at work.

Third party debt order

Cash flow problems often lie at the root of people's failure to pay judgment debts. Some debtors are owed money themselves. If your debtor is owed money, you can require that person to pay the money directly to you. Alternatively, the debtor may have bank accounts with money in them and these banks can be required to pass the money directly to you.

To obtain the order you need to make an application for a third party debt order by completing Form N349 and sending it to the court with the correct fee. Up-to-date information on the fee charged may be obtained from the Court Service website or from the court office. Remember that if it is a bank or building society account you are attaching, full account details will be needed. If you have an old cheque from the debtor, you can obtain the account number, sort code and so on. If you do not provide full details, you may end up having to pay the third party to search its records.

The application for the order is put before a judge who can make an interim third party debt order. The interim order will require the third party (the debtor's own creditor) to retain a specific amount of money in order to pay the debt. This means that the third party is not allowed to make payments from the account that would reduce the balance to less than the debt and a further sum must be retained to cover the creditor's costs. At the same time the judge orders a hearing to take place to make the order final. The hearing for the final order must be at least 28 days after the interim order was made. The court serves the interim order on the third party not less than 21 days prior to the hearing for the final order. In order to give the third party time to freeze the accounts before the debtor attempts to move his assets, the judgment debtor is served with the interim order not less than seven days after the interim order is made. The debtor has an opportunity to oppose the making of a final third party debt order at the next hearing. Once the order is made final the third party must pay the sum ordered by the court to you.

However, debtors can have multiple accounts. If your debtor is good at moving money around, it can be difficult to identify an account with money in it at the time the interim order is served on the third party. So, do not warn your debtor that you will seek this order in case he attempts to transfer his assets elsewhere. The interim order operates only once at the moment at which it is served. If there is nothing in an account at the moment of the service of the interim order, you will not recover any money.

An example of a request for third party debt order can be found on the following pages.

Charging order

The biggest asset most people possess is their own home. So if your debtor owns his own property, you can attempt to enforce your debt by attaching your debt to his property. This means that if the debtor wishes to sell his property, he will not be able to do so without paying you. After you have obtained a charging order you can enforce the order by applying to the court for an order of sale. However, you will need legal advice as to whether the court is likely to enforce the order by sale. If the debtor has

Application for Third Party Debt Order Form N349

Application for third party debt order

In the

Claim No.

Appn. No.

Claimant

Defendant

Third Party

The [claimant] [defendant] ('the judgment creditor') applies for an order that the third party pay to the judgment creditor the debt which the third party owes to the [defendant] [claimant] ('the judgment debtor') (or so much of it as is necessary to discharge the amount owing under the judgment or order given on   20   [by the   in claim no.   ] and the costs of this application).

1. **Judgment debtor**
    The judgment debtor is
    whose address is

                                                                Postcode

2. **Judgment debt**
    The judgment or order required the judgment debtor to pay £   (including any costs and interest). The amount now due is £   [which includes further interest].
    ☐ £   of the instalments due under the judgment or order has fallen due and remains unpaid.

    ☐ The judgment or order did not provide for payment by instalments.

3. **Third party**
    The third party is within England and Wales and owes money to (or holds money to the credit of) the judgment debtor.

    The third party is a bank or building society.
    Its name is
    Its head office address in England and Wales is:

    The branch at which the account is held is
    ☐ not known

    ☐ the
        whose address is

    The account number is   The sort code is
    ☐ not known   ☐ not known
    ☐   ☐

Application for Third Party Debt Order Form N349 (continued)

[The third party is not a bank or building society.

☐ the third party is

whose address in England and Wales is

4. **Other persons' interests**
The persons (in addition to the judgment debtor) who have a claim to the money owed by the third party are
☐ None

☐ The following: *(names and address(es))*

Information known about each person's claim:

5. **Sources and grounds of information**
The judgment creditor knowns or believes that the information in section 3 and 4 is correct because:

6. **Other applications**
In respect of the judgment debt,
☐ the judgment creditor has made no other applications for third party debt orders.
☐ the judgment creditor has already made the following application(s) for third party debt order:
Details of application(s)

Third party's name
Address

Postcode

Statement of Truth
*I believe (the judgment creditor believes) that the facts stated in this application form are true.
*I am duly authorised by the judgment creditor to sign this statement

signed _____ date _____
*(Judgment creditor)(Litigation friend *(where judgment creditor is a child or a patient)*)(Judgment creditor's solicitor)
delete as appropriate
Full name _____
Name of judgment creditor's solicitor's firm _____
position or office held _____ *(if signing on behalf of a firm or company)*

Judgment creditor's or
judgment creditor's
solicitor's address to
which documents
should be sent.

Postcode

	if applicable
Ref. no.	
fax no.	
DX no.	
e-mail	
Tel. no.	

young children living with him in the property, the court has the power to suspend the order for sale until the children are grown up. The process of applying for an order of sale is more technically complicated too, so you may need to consider taking legal advice. However, if you wish to apply for a charging order, you will also need to do a search of the property register at HM Land Registry. This is because you need the title number of the property you wish to charge. You may have obtained this information if the court has orally examined the debtor. If not, visit www.landregister online.gov.uk and carry out a title search. There is a modest fee for this service. Alternatively, you can telephone 020 7917 8888 for more information.

The interim order

There are two stages to obtaining a charging order. The first stage is where you apply for an interim charging order. To do this, you complete Form N379. You will see at once that there are eight parts to the form. Parts 1 and 2 are easy. Part 3 refers to the title number of the property. Notice that you need to attach an office copy of the Land Register entry for the property you wish to charge. Parts 4 and 5 are self-explanatory, but part 6 needs care. The title search you carried out will reveal the names of anyone with a legal share of the sale proceeds of the property, but it may not reveal the existence of others with a potential interest in the property. For example, if you know the debtor has an elderly relative who has lived in the property with him for many years, you need to enter the name. Insert it under 'the following persons have or may have an interest in the property...' This is so the court can serve a copy of the interim charging order on such persons in due course. When the form is completed, send it to the court with the correct fee. As the fees change from time to time you need to check the amount with the court. The application will be put before a judge.

If he is satisfied that the forms are correctly completed and the rules have been followed, the judge will make an interim charging order. He will also fix a hearing date for the final order to give the debtor an opportunity to appear and object to the order. Copies of the interim order, together with the application and supporting documents, are served on the debtor by the court. Service must be not less than 21 days of the hearing date for the final order. The effect of the interim order is to prevent the debtor attempting to sell his share of the property before the hearing of the final order. But you must register the interim order as a land charge with the Land Charges Department of HM Land Registry in Plymouth, if the land is unregistered land. If the land is registered, the interim order must be registered with HM Land Registry. Look up your telephone directory to find your local registry. Alternatively, visit www.landregisteronline.gov.uk.

An example of Form N379 can be found on the following pages.

The final order

At the hearing the court may either dismiss the application or make the order final. If the order is made final, you can apply for sale of the land. However, this application is more technically complex and you will need legal advice to take this step effectively. Leaflet EX325 is available at www.hmcourts-service.gov.uk or County Court offices. It gives guidance on obtaining third party debt orders and charging orders.

Bankruptcy order

You can issue a bankruptcy petition against your debtor. The effect of the order is to prevent the debtor from dealing with his own assets. All his financial dealings become subject to restrictions imposed by the court. Debtors use this method of enforcement as a means of coercing the debtor into paying up. However, it is often ineffective and it is also technically complicated. The expense of paying a deposit (currently £390) to the receiver should deter a judgment creditor from taking this step unless the debtor has substantial assets. For information on how to do this, visit www.insolvency.gov.uk and follow the links from there.

Winding up order

When a company is unable to pay its debts, creditors may apply to wind up the company. The effect of the order is to force the company to cease

Application for a Charging Order on Land or Property Form N379

Application
for charging order
on land or property

In the
BEDFORD COUNTY COURT

Claim No.

BDF066523

Appn. No.

Lawrence Harding trading as Harding Domestic Roofing

Claimant

Jason Gornal

Defendant

The [claimant] [defendant] ('the judgment creditor') applies for an order imposing a charge on the interest of the [defendant] [claimant] ('the judgment debtor') in the land or property mentioned below to secure payment of the amount owing under the judgment or order given on 31st March   20 06   [by the Bedford County Court   in claim no. BDF066523   ].

1.   Judgment debtor
The judgment debtor is
whose address is
6 Fennel Lane Bedford

Postcode   MK43 6GL

2.   Judgment debt
The judgment or order required the judgment debtor to pay £ 4194.60   (including any costs and interest). The amount now owing is £ 4239.50   [which includes further interest payable on the judgment debt].

☐ £   of the instalments due under the judgment or order has fallen due and remains unpaid.

☑ The judgment or order did not provide for payment by instalments.

3.   The land or property
The address of the land or property upon which it is sought to impose a to charge is
6 Fennel Lane Bedford MK43 6GL

[the title to which is registered at H. M. Land Registry under Title No. BD25785
An Office Copy of the Land Register entries for this title is attached.]

4.   Judgment debtor's interest in the land or property
The judgment debtor is:
☐ the sole owner   ☑ a joint owner   ☐ a beneficiary under a trust

☑ This is shown by the Office Copy Land Register entries attached.

☐ The judgment creditor believes this to be so because

N379 Application for charging order on land or property (03.02)   *Printed on behalf of The Court Service*

Application for a Charging Order on Land or Property Form N379 (continued)

5.   Other creditors

☐ The judgment creditor does not know of any other creditors of the judgment debtor.

☑ The judgment creditor knows of the following other creditors of the judgment debtor:
(names and addresses and, if known, nature of debt and amount)

6.   Other persons to be served

☑ No other person has an interest in the property (including any co-owners, trustees and persons with rights of occupation).

☐ The following persons have or may have an interest in the property:
(name and address and, if known, nature of interest)

7.   Further information

The judgment creditor asks the court to take account of the following:

8.   Sources of information *(Complete only where the judgment creditor is a firm or a company or other corporation)*
[The information in this application is given [by me] [by   of
                                                who is the   of the
judgment creditor] after making proper enquiry of all persons within the judgment creditor's
organisation who might have knowledge of the facts.]

Statement of Truth

*I believe (the judgment creditor believes) that the facts stated in this application form are true.
*I am duly authorised by the judgment creditor to sign this statement

signed _____ date 7 June 2006 _____

*(Judgment creditor)(Litigation friend *(where judgment creditor is a child or a patient)*)(Judgment creditor's solicitor)
delete as appropriate
Full name _____
Name of judgment creditor's solicitor's firm _____
position or office held _____ *(if signing on behalf of a firm or company)*

Judgment creditor's or judgment creditor's solicitor's address to which documents should be sent.	Lawrence Harding trading as Harding Domestic Roofing 11 Heston Road Bedford Postcode MK15 8BW		*if applicable*
		Ref. no.	06/247
		fax no.	
		DX no.	
		e-mail	hdb@Bestnet.co.uk
		Tel. no.	

trading and to sell all its assets so that its debts can be paid off. In reality, it is really a way of coercing the company to pay its debts. If a company is genuinely unable to pay its debts, the creditors are unlikely to gain much from a winding up petition. This is because the debtor's bank, HM Revenue & Customs and other secure creditors get the first bite at the cherry. By the time its debts are satisfied there is often nothing left for the unsecured creditors. If there is, the unsecured creditors share what is left in varying proportions. An unsecured creditor may end up with ten pence for every pound he was owed, or more, or less.

The cost of applying for a winding up petition is prohibitively expensive and is probably not justified for small claims. If you are determined to issue a winding up petition, you should carry out a search of the Register of Judgments, Orders and Fines to see if the company has other debtors and a company search to find out if it has any assets. You also need to ascertain whether another winding up petition has already been issued. To do this, visit www.insolvency.gov.uk. However, do be aware that it is not a procedure for 'DIY' and you will need assistance from a qualified lawyer.

Enforcing judgment by Money Claim Online

The only method of enforcement that can be done online currently is requesting the issue of a warrant of execution. If you have obtained judgment against a debtor using Money Claim Online (MCOL), then it is simple to log onto the system by confirming your user ID and password. The system enables users to select the claim they wish to enforce and then to select the 'warrant of execution' option. The form requesting issue of the warrant is the same N323 and is completed in the same way electronically as by hand. However, there is one small difference. If the court judgment ordered instalment payments, the request must be for a minimum of £50.

No request is issued until the correct payment has been made electronically. Once payment has been made, MCOL issues the request for issue of warrant. If the request was made before 9am, it does so the same day. If the request was made after 9am, it issues the request the next day the court is open.

How is the warrant enforced?

The court sends the warrants electronically to the bailiffs of the defendant's home court. The bailiffs keep the Northampton Court notified since the administration of the debt remains with the Northampton County Court. Users can check up on progress online.

Glossary

Acknowledgment of service	The act of the defendant in completing and returning Form N9B to the court.
Adjudication	A process by which a person is appointed to decide a dispute between the parties. It is not regulated by the court rules, but is subject to the rules of natural justice.
Allocation form	Form N149, used for cases likely to be allocated to the small claims track.
Arbitration	A process by which a privately appointed judge or arbitrator assesses and then decides a claim. There are a number of arbitration schemes including that run by ABTA, as well as schemes that have been regulated by Act of Parliament.
Assets	The property of an individual or organisation that has a sale value and is potentially available to satisfy debt.
Attachment of Earnings Order	An order by which an employer is obliged by the court to deduct a fixed sum from the employee's salary or wages each week or month and then to pass that sum to the County Court Bulk Centre in Northampton.
Bailiff	An officer of the court employed to enter the premises of a debtor, to seize goods and sell them in order to raise enough cash to pay the debtor's creditors.

Bailment	An agreement, either express or implicit, that a person in receipt of the property of another will look after it. This means that the person who receives the property is obliged to protect it from damage, destruction or theft (e.g. the dry cleaner who receives a suit must return it undamaged to the owner after it has been cleaned and the bill paid).
Balance of probability	*See* civil standard of proof.
Bankrupt	The old word to describe a person who was personally insolvent and against whom there was an order of bankruptcy.
Bond	A sum of money which is security for the performance of a contractual obligation.
Bondholder	A person or organisation who receives the bond and holds it upon certain terms and conditions on behalf of another. For example, domestic landlords obliged by statute to hand over tenants' deposits to a bondholder under the Housing Act 2004.
Cause of action	A legal ground for making a claim (e.g. breach of contract).
Charging order	An order securing the sum owed to a creditor against the assets of the debtor, usually a property.
Civil Court Practice Rules	The rules governing the conduct of civil claims in the courts.
Civil standard of proof	The claimant must prove the claim on the balance of probability, i.e. that it is more likely than not that the claim is true.
Claim	A request to the court that a judgment be granted against the defendant for an actionable wrong on the legal grounds set out in the Claim Form.
Claim Form	The N1 Form that must be completed in order to begin a claim in the County Court.

Claim number	The identification number allocated by the court to a claim and inserted into the right-hand corner of the Claim Form.
Claim Production Centre (CPC)	The office in the centre of Northampton that carries out the volume issue of Claim Forms for bulk users of the system, such as debt recovery agencies and the debt recovery departments of solicitors' firms. Claims are issued in the name of the Northampton County Court or the court the user requests.
Claimant	A person who is making a claim that has been issued by the court.
Closed questions	Questions that suggest what the answer should be or which close down the available options (e.g. the often quoted 'When did you stop beating your wife?').
Compensation	An award of a sum of money designed to put right the loss and expense suffered by a party as a result of the actions or omissions of another party.
Complaints procedure	A formal process adopted by many organisations to investigate allegations of poor products and/or services and/or misconduct.
Conciliation	A process by which the conciliator actively attempts to broker settlement of a dispute between two or more parties by investigating the facts and positions of the parties. The conciliator will make recommendations and attempt to reconcile parties. Mediation does not attempt to alter the positions of the parties nor to reconcile them or make recommendations. Practitioners describe conciliation as a less formal process than mediation.
Contract	An oral or written agreement, intended to be legally binding, which commits the parties to it to comply with various duties and obligations.

Contract 'under seal'	A contract in which the parties to it authenticate their consent by the use of seals (now self-adhesive red circles).
Costs	The fees charged by the court for the use of its services and the cost of paying witnesses to attend court.
Counterclaim	A claim by a defendant against a claimant.
County Court Bulk Centre (CCBC)	Also located in the same office block as CPC in the centre of Northampton. The CCBC processes requests for judgments and the issue of warrants of execution.
County Courts	The network of civil courts that administer civil claims.
Court fees	The fees charged by a court to carry out administrative acts necessary to bring a case to trial.
Creditor	A person owed money by a debtor.
Cross-examination	The process by which the credibility of evidence given in chief is tested.
Damages	Another name for money or compensation for a civil wrong.
Debt recovery agency	An organisation dedicated to recovering its clients' debts.
Debtor	A person who owes money to a creditor.
Default judgment	The judgment entered by a court against a defendant who has not acknowledged service of the claim or notified the court of his defence.
Defence	The facts and matters upon which a defendant relies to escape the obligation to pay a claim.
Defendant	The person against whom a claimant makes a claim.
Directions	The procedural steps ordered by a court to bring a claim to trial.
Dispute	A disagreement over the legal consequences of actions and omissions.

District Judge	The judge of the County Court that conducts most small claims
Enforcement	The process by which a judgment creditor secures payment of the judgment debt.
Evidence	Relevant oral statements, documents and opinions that the court is prepared to consider in arriving at a decision.
Examination-in-chief	The process by which a witness gives the court evidence.
Exclusion clause	A term of a contract reducing or excluding liability for breach of contract.
Exemption clause	A term of a contract reducing or excluding liability for certain eventualities.
Expert witness	A person whose training, work experience and specialist knowledge qualifies him to give evidence to the court.
Express term	A term of a contract that is expressly agreed between the contracting parties.
Fast track	The route by which claims over £5,000 are heard in the County Court.
Fit for the purpose	Goods are suitable for the purpose for which they are commonly supplied.
Implied term	A term of a contract that is not expressly agreed between parties to an agreement but which may still govern the contract.
Insolvent	A person or organisation that is unable to pay its debts as they fall due.
Interest payments	Compensation awarded to a claimant against a defendant for keeping the claimant out of his money.
Issue date	The date on which the court enters a claim number on Form N1 and inserts the date in the right-hand corner.
Issuing the claim	The formal acceptance of a claim by the court, by the administrative act of entering a claim

	number on a Claim Form and notifying the defendant.
Judgment	The declaration of a court upon the claims of parties to a court action.
Landlord	A person who permits the tenant exclusive possession of a property, for a fixed period of time under a tenancy agreement or lease, in return for rent.
Letter before action	A letter warning the party to whom it is sent of a legal claim that will begin within a fixed period of time unless certain actions are taken.
Limitation clause	A contract clause that reduces the compensation that may be claimed.
Limited company	An association incorporated under the Companies Acts whose liabilities are limited in the event of the company becoming insolvent.
Limited liability partnership	A form of partnership by which the liabilities of the partnership are limited.
Litigant in person	A person who conducts his own claim and represents himself in court.
Loss	The sums of money that represent the financial damage sustained by a person as a result of the civil wrongs of another.
Mediation	The process by which a mediator assists in the resolution of disputes.
Mediator	A person trained to facilitate the resolution of disputes.
Mitigation of loss	The duty upon a claimant to do what he can to reduce the loss he suffers.
Money Claim Online (MCOL)	The online claim service operated by the Court Service.
N1 Form	The Claim Form needed to start a claim in the County Court.
N1A	The form containing the notes to assist users of Claim Form N1.

N1C	Notes to assist the defendant to reply to a Claim Form.
N9	Acknowledgment of service form.
N9A	Admission form for a specific amount of money.
N9B	Defence form for disputing part or all of a claim for a specific amount of money and setting out the grounds of the defence.
N9C	Admission of unspecific amount of money.
N9D	Defence to claim for an unspecific amount of money.
N20	Witness summons.
N30	Judgment for claimant in default.
N30(1)	Judgment for claimant by acceptance of claim.
N30(2)	Judgment for claimant after trial or determination.
N149	Allocation Questionnaire.
N157	Notice of allocation to the small claims track.
N205A	Notice of issue of Claim Form for specific sum of money and request for judgment form.
N205B	Notice of issue of Claim Form for unspecific sum of money and request for judgment form.
N215	Certificate of service.
N225	Request for entry of judgment where claim is specific.
N227	Request for entry of judgment on unspecific claim.
N244	Application form for general request to the court.
N316	Application for debtor to attend court to be questioned as to his liabilities and assets.
N323	Request for issue of warrant of execution.
N337	Request for attachment of earnings order.
N349	Request for a third party debt order.

N379	Application for a charging order on land or property.
Negligence	The commission of an act or omission, in breach of a duty of care, that causes loss and damage to another.
Negligent omission	The failure to carry out an act that ought to have been carried out to avoid liability for negligence.
'Next friend'	A person who acts as the representative of another, who is unable to represent himself in legal proceedings (e.g. a child or minor or person lacking capacity to represent himself).
Open questions	Questions that are a genuine attempt at dialogue and explanation and therefore do not suggest the answer.
Overriding objective	A statement of the guiding principles governing the application of the court rules to cases.
Particulars of Claim	The details of a claim that appear on page 2 of Form N1.
Penalty clause	A term of an agreement that imposes an obligation on one party to make payment of a pre-determined sum. However, in the event that the other party fails to meet its own obligations, there is no such obligation.
Personal guarantees	An agreement that a person who has no legal obligations under a contract will be liable to pay compensation for breach of that contract.
Personal injuries	Physical or psychological harm suffered by a person as a result of the wrongful action or failure to act of another.
Personal service	The service of a court document upon a person by another person.
Register of Judgments, Orders and Fines	The official list of judgments of the court.
Rescission	An order by which a court declares a contract to be of no effect and by which the contracting

	parties are returned to their pre-contractual positions.
Response Pack	The bundle of documents sent to a defendant by the County Court following the issue of a claim.
'Satisfactory' quality	A description of goods supplied or sold that are of the quality to be expected of goods of that particular kind.
Seal	A stamp proving that a document is genuine. Some contract documents are still made 'under seal'. The use of wax seals has long been replaced with rubber stamps.
Secure creditors	A creditor that has ensured it will receive priority in the payment of a debtor's debts over the unsecured creditors as a result of a legal agreement between creditor and debtor or as a result of an Act of Parliament.
Service	The process by which a court brings a claim to the attention of a defendant.
Setting aside judgment	An order by which the court withdraws a judgment it has entered so that the defendant may dispute a claim.
Settlement	The pre-trial agreement of a dispute.
Small Claims Court	A court hearing a claim allocated to the small claims track.
Statement of truth	A declaration that the contents of a document are true.
Strike out	An order of the court by which a claim or a defence or a counterclaim is made ineffective and which entitles the other side to an entry of judgment in their favour.
Summons	The old name for the Claim Form issued by the County Court.
Tenant	A person who has exclusive possession of property, owned by another, in accordance with

	the terms of an agreement regulating the terms of that possession.
Terms	The duties and obligations of parties to an agreement.
Third Party Debt Orders	A court order requiring a creditor of the debtor to make payment of a judgment debt out of assets of the debtor in its possession.
Trespass to property	Any act that unjustifiably interferes with land possessed by another land.
Unfair Contracts Terms Act 1977	An enactment of the UK government striking down certain types of exclusion clauses and making the rest subject to a test of reasonableness.
Unfair Terms in Consumer Contracts Regulations 1999	An enactment of a European Directive giving consumers rights of redress against the use of unfair terms in consumer contracts.
Unincorporated association	An organisation that has no legal personality, is not a limited company, partnership nor an individual (e.g. most clubs, societies and associations, political parties).
Unsecured creditor	A creditor whose debt is not secured against the assets of a company.
Usher	A person who assists in the administration and operation of the courts.
Vexation and inconvenience	A form of psychological suffering which the law will compensate if it is consequent on real physical inconvenience.
Vexatious litigant	A person who takes legal proceedings although the legal grounds for so doing barely exist.
Warrant of execution	An order permitting a bailiff to enter the premises of the debtor to remove and sell goods to satisfy a judgment debt.
Warranty	A guarantee of the condition or performance of goods and services. To fail to abide by the warranty is a breach of warranty.

Witness	A person who gives oral or written evidence to a court.
Witness expenses	The compensation a court awards a witness for attending court to give evidence.
Witness statement	A written record of the evidence of a witness.
Wrongful	An act that is contrary to law.

Appendix

Useful contacts

Better Payment Practice Campaign

www.payontime.co.uk

For information on The Late Payment of Commercial Debts (Interest) Act 1998.

Business Link

www.businesslink.gov.uk/debt

A useful site where you can obtain information on how to recover your debts or speak to a Business Link adviser on 0845 600 9006.

Organisations that offer complaints resolution

Air Transport Users Council

www.auc.org.uk

Complaints handling.

Association of British Travel Agents

www.abta.com

Arbitration scheme.

Association of Independent Tour Operators

www.aito.co.uk

Low-cost independent dispute settlement service.

Association of Master Upholsterers and Soft Furnishers

www.upholsterers.co.uk

Mediation and arbitration scheme.

Community Legal Service Direct

www.clsdirect.org.uk

Advice site.

Domestic Appliance Service Association

www.dasa.org.uk

Complaints procedure with mediation and arbitration scheme.

Federation of Master Builders

www.fmb.org.uk

Complaints resolution process.

Financial Ombudsman Scheme

www.financial-ombudsman.org.uk

Provides consumers with free independent advice for resolving disputes with a financial firm and includes a formal complaints procedure.

Internet Services Providers' Association, UK

www.ispa.org.uk

For complaints procedures.

Ombudsman for Estate Agents Scheme

www.oea.co.uk

Complaints procedure.

Qualitas National Conciliation Service

www.qualitas.uk.com

Conciliation and adjudication scheme.

Radio Electrical and Television Retailers' Association Ltd

www.retra.co.uk

An independent conciliation panel.

Retail Motor Industry Federation

www.rmif.co.uk

Complaints about used cars, repairs and servicing in England and Wales referred to The National Conciliation Service, 9 North Street, Rugby CV21 2AB.

Index

This index covers all sections of the book. Forms and leaflets are indexed by 'N' and 'EX' numbers (covered in greater detail in the Glossary); principal forms are also indexed by their name.

limitations 144
Response Pack 72, 74-6, 137, 142, 148
rights 1

S
Sale and Supply of Goods Act 1994 45-7, 48, 128, 143, 144-6, 147
Sale of Goods Act 1979 45-7, 143, 144-5
sales of property, charging orders on 170, 173-4, 175-6
salespeople 45, 143
satellite dishes 154
sealing 50, 69, 71, 77, 187
searches, title 173
seating 115
secured creditors 187
  unsecured creditors and 177
self-employment 32-4
  representation 10-11
service of claims 149, 150
  by correspondence 71, 148, 153
  by email and fax 72
  by personal service 71-2
  scope 71
  see also Acknowledgment of Service Form
settlements 32-4, 85, 142
shops 19-20
signatures
  by authorised people 68
  entry of name as 133
  by self 68, 92
site visits 88
size of claims 2-3, 8-9, 60, 86
Small Claims Courts 7, 58, 60
  disputed jurisdiction 151
  formality 3, 11, 110, 115
  representation 9-11
  scope 8-9
  transferral 82, 85-6
  see also individual terms
societies 42-3
software, as faulty 46, 145
sole traders 40
solicitors 1
  as authorised people 68